The Shopfloor Politi
New Technology

The Shopfloor Politics of New Technology

Barry Wilkinson

Heinemann Educational Books

To K.J.

Heinemann Educational Books Ltd
22 Bedford Square, London WC1B 3HH
LONDON EDINBURGH MELBOURNE AUCKLAND
HONG KONG SINGAPORE KUALA LUMPUR NEW DELHI
IBADAN NAIROBI JOHANNESBURG
EXETER (NH) KINGSTON PORT OF SPAIN

First published 1983

British Library Cataloguing in Publication Data

Wilkinson, Barry
The shopfloor politics of new technology.
1. Technological innovation—Social aspects—Great Britain 2. Technological innovation—Economic aspects—Great Britain 3. Great Britain—Industry
I. Title
338'.06 HC79.T4

ISBN 0-435-82950-5
ISBN 0-435-82051-3 Pbk

Typeset by Inforum Ltd, Portsmouth
Printed in Great Britain by Biddles Ltd, Guildford, Surrey

Contents

Acknowledgements

My greatest debt is to Professor Ernest Braun of the University of Aston's Technology Policy Unit. His close attention to my work and constant encouragement made this book possible.

Many other people provided valuable help in reading and correcting drafts of chapters and passing valuable comments at various stages of the research. It is not possible to list them all, but particularly important in their own ways were the following:

– Harry Scarbrough, especially for our discussions and arguments on the more theoretical aspects of technical change.

– Dr. Russell Moseley, who helped my formulation of the research aims in the early stages, and provided valuable comments on the drafts of many chapters.

– Professor John Child, whose interest in, and comments on my work helped me keep sight of the basic aims.

– Dr. Roy Rothwell, especially for his comments on the concluding chapters.

I would like to thank the Science Research Council for their funding of the project, and hope they would agree their money has not been wasted. Also all students and staff of the Technology Policy Unit, not only for providing a healthy academic climate, but also for providing a felicific base for what was occasionally a lonely undertaking.

Finally, I would like to thank my wife Karen, for putting up with a research project over the last couple of years, and in particular for contributing many hours of hard work in helping me meet the deadlines.

Preface

While the literature on the social aspects of the new technology is extensive, few researchers have addressed themselves to exactly what is happening on the shopfloors of British industry as more and more firms find uses for microelectronics. This book looks at the qualitative employment aspects of new technology – the ways in which the organisation of work is changing, especially the changing nature of jobs and skills.

Most especially the book is an exploration of the social and political processes involved in the introduction of new technology to the shopfloor. Through a series of case studies of the application of microelectronics to batch manufacture, it attempts to uncover the ways in which the values and interests of managers, engineers and workers profoundly influence the choice and use of technology, and thus the work organisation which emerges.

Previous analyses have tended to treat new technology as if it had 'impacts' on work organisation – especially skills – which are inevitable in particular technical and economic circumstances. It is in opposition to this view that technical change is here treated as a matter for social choice and political negotiation, the various interested parties to the change being shown to attempt to incorporate their own interests into the technical and social organisation of work.

The first two chapters provide the theoretical introduction, though they are not intended as a thorough review of the literature. Rather, they aim to sensitise the reader to the debate which has gone on so far, and to outline my own perspective. Thus chapter one draws out the inadequacies of previous theoretical and empirical work, while chapter two – in many ways the pivotal chapter – uses this critique as a basis for the development of an alternative approach centred on the *politics* of technical change. Technological choice and the establishment of working practices are shown to be *contested*, rather than the specific consequences of a system outside the control of actors and interest groups.

The case studies themselves were carried out between the autumn of 1979 and spring 1981 in the West Midlands – appropriately, Britain's 'manufacturing base'. They are presented in chapters three to eight as a set of 'episodes' of innovation, attention being focused upon the ways interested individuals and groups attempt to impose their own designs at the various stages of the process.

Chapter nine compares and contrasts the case studies to illustrate the social and political dynamics involved in the introduction of new technology. It shows how the various stages of design, trial, debugging, etc., provide junctures at which people intervene to influence the process of technical change and its effects, and it explains how choices are made and bargaining carried on. Finally, chapter ten, the second of two concluding chapters, brings to light and assesses the policy issues which the research uncovered, and which must be faced by managers, engineers and trade unions.

In concentrating on a vital problem area, this book transcends the boundaries not only between the various conventional disciplines of sociology, economics, engineering, etc., but also between 'theory' and 'practice'. Thus it is hoped that practitioners as well as the various students of industry will make use of the research. It has important things to say to both.

1 Economic and Social Aspects of the New Technology

Work remains the most central and important institution in British society. Patterns of shiftworking, payment systems and levels of remuneration, workgroup relations, and most especially the tasks we do, all affect our modern experience of work. With the introduction of new technology these patterns of work organisation are changing – often in radical ways – and it is the purpose of this book to examine what those changes may be and, perhaps more importantly, the processes by which they come about. This chapter serves as an introduction by outlining the character of the new microelectronics technology, and its implications for work in manufacturing industry. Chapter two will develop the particular theoretical perspective to be used in the analysis of the case studies.

Automation and the Microelectronics Revolution

The debate on 'automation' and its social impacts has gone on for many years now, with particular attention arising with the first major uses of the computer in the 1950's. Recently, with the advent of semiconductor electronics, the debate has been sparked off again, with a host of commentators predicting and forecasting all sorts of impacts on working lives, on leisure patterns, and so on.

What microelectronics has done is, first, to decrease both the physical size and the economic costs of electronic devices – including computers – and, second, to extend the range of processes which are amenable to automation. Applications are now found in virtually every sector of the economy, and costs have reduced so dramatically that for many applications they can be afforded by even the smallest firms. Many commentators are thus hailing a revolution in industry and commerce which is likely to have repercussions equal in magnitude to the industrial revolution itself.[1]

At a 'macro' level, the two main social issues raised are first, the likely impact on overall employment levels, and second, the rise and decline in the relative importance of the various sectors of the economy as sources of employment. Predictions of future levels of unemployment caused by the displacement effects of the new technology vary enormously, and the measurement of these effects is fraught with difficulties. However, there is general agreement that any unemployment caused by microelectronics will in the long term be less serious than that which might be caused by the failure to automate, because of the enormous competitive advantages which are at stake. In short, as long as British industry competes with that of other countries, it must make use of the chip or face the chop.[2] The problem is then, how best to ensure the even distribution of the benefits of the new technology, and such issues as possibilities for work sharing or for shortening the working week are thus being raised. Traditional ideas about unemployment must be brought into question, and indeed so must the whole work ethic which has dominated the Western world for the last few centuries.

Associated with the debate on the effect on overall employment levels is that about the rise and decline of economic sectors. Manufacturing industry has required less and less labour for decades due to advances in production technology, but so far the surplus labour created has been taken up by a growth in total manufacturing output and by new and growing service industries – health, education, finance, insurance, recreation, etc. These services are held to need expansion to absorb the displaced labour associated with microelectronics, though it is questionable whether or not this will occur.[3]

Related to these two issues is the debate on the changing nature of the labour force which may be brought about by the rise of a service economy. To summarise briefly: the central question of the debate is whether the growing service economy represents – as Daniel Bell[4] suggests – a radical divergence from traditional industry, or whether it is in fact mainly an extension of the existing order – as is argued by Jonathan Gershuny.[5] That is, are the new services socially-oriented – as with medicine and education – or are they, like banking and insurance, aids to the efficiency of material production? One of the latest contributions to the debate comes from Clive Jenkins and Barrie Sherman, who urge the development of the 'pink-collar' sector to absorb displaced labour. 'Pink-collar' work is in the 'person-to-person' services such as hairdressing, entertainment, restaurants, and so on, as well as medicine and education. Generally, not being amenable to automation (unlike banking, insurance, etc.), they could bring many employment opportunities.[6]

All these are major issues which are beyond the scope of this book. Our own interests in the microelectronics revolution are in the more detailed qualitative aspects of employment, and this chapter will focus on the implications of change at the level of the office and factory floors.[7]

Applications in Manufacturing Industry

For the general employment issues mentioned above it is difficult not to talk about the effects of microelectronics *as a whole*, and, no doubt, for some purposes this may be highly desirable. However, discussion of the qualitative employment aspects of applications at the point of production can easily lead to confusion if the type of automation is not distinguished. For instance, Blauner[8] and Bright[9] come to very different conclusions. While Blauner claims that automation demands more democratic, autonomous and responsible work activities than conventional technologies, Bright holds that automation leads to more centralised control, closer supervision, and more specialised tasks. One of the main reasons is that the authors use exemplars from different industries – Blauner is referring to continuous process production while Bright refers to the engineering industry. Thus at the very least, we might distinguish between 'continuous process production', 'mass production', and 'office automation'. Different 'impacts' have been recorded in each of these sectors.[10]

This is not to say that impacts *within* sectors are necessarily uniform. On the contrary, one of the basic propositions of this book will be that *variations* in effects are possible because of independent social and political influences. But it is nonetheless vital to recognise the broad differences in automation when discussing effects. Our case studies are mainly of *batch* production in various branches of the engineering industry, and the specific character of automation of this type of manufacturing process will now be discussed.

Until the advent of sophisticated electronics and computers after the second world war, the automation of production processes could generally be described as 'hard' automation, where making processes automatic involved the use of stops, cams, and so on, so that human intervention was not required. This type of machinery has its origins in the nineteenth century, and continues to be important today. Its use is limited, however, to mass and large batch production, since once set up, it is normally a very costly and time-consuming business to adapt the machinery to even slight changes in the product. Indeed, product changes may even mean the scrapping of whole sets of machinery which are no use for any other purpose. Thus many sectors of the engineering industry, where small and medium sized batches predominate, have found little use for these conventional automatic machines, and by far the majority of batch production processes remain manually controlled.

Today, however, automation of batch production is on the increase, and automation even for very small batches or 'one-offs' (single components) is becoming economically viable. This is because of the advent of electronic and computer-controlled machinery, where control of the production of a component lies not in the physical hardware of stops and cams, nor in the human machine operator, but rather in the programmable software of the machine's electronic control system. The use of 'soft' automation for small batches is made possible by the flexibility which comes with programmable control – re-programming or re-setting is easy compared with adapting hardware. The increasing sophistication and decreasing costs of electronic control systems due to the availability of microelectronics has enormously extended the range of feasible applications. Virtually every sector of manufacturing industry which uses multipurpose machinery is either already under competitive pressure, or likely soon to come under pressure to make use of the new control devices.

Soft automation arose after World War II, the first applications coming in the form of numerically controlled (NC) machine tools in the metal working industry. Electronic control devices are, however, equally applicable to other, similar, multi-purpose machinery, and as well as machine tools, the applications observed in the case studies included die-casting machinery, plating equipment, mechanical handling equipment, a large press for the extrusion of metal, and rubber moulding machinery. Partly because of the central importance of machine tools in manufacturing industry, and the vast numbers in use, attention has been focused on automation here rather than on any other machinery; and our discussion will thus focus on numerical control as a detailed exemplar of soft automation for batch production. It should therefore be borne in mind that very similar issues are raised by electronic control devices applied to the whole range of machinery mentioned above.

Applications of Microelectronics in Batch Production

The development and application of numerical control for machine tools began in the late 1940's and early 1950's, and with the increasing sophistication of electronics in the 1960's began to spread rapidly throughout the engineering industry. The aircraft industry was the first major user, but NC usage has now spread to all sectors. The NC market in the UK has grown by around 9% per annum since 1971, and all existing NC machinery in 1978 represented about 1.5% of all machine tools.[11] It is expected that cheap microprocessors will lead to a more rapid increase in market share in the near future.[12] The UK has been slow to take up NC, and the reasons why have been discussed in detail.[13]

Basically, with NC, information on the size and shape of a component is fed into a control device – the information bearer normally being a paper or magnetic tape. This information is then passed via a series of electro-mechanical devices (the machine's 'servo-mechanism') which can run the machine. The technical advantages of this system over conventional (manual *and* automatic) control systems can be many and varied. Most importantly: pre-coding of the job means that metal cutting is made easier and that the tool itself can be in more constant use; the tape can be filed and recalled whenever needed, and minor design modifications can easily be made. Compared with conventional automatic machine tools flexibility is greatly increased. The cost per standard hour of the new machine is higher than that of conventional machines due to higher depreciation (NC is more expensive) and higher support costs (especially maintenance and programming), but these costs can be offset by higher output, and thus decreased cost per component, if utilisation is kept high.[14]

More recently 'computer numerical control' (CNC) has been developed, where a powerful mini- or micro-computer is installed on the machine tool itself. With this system the programme is read only once for a whole batch of components, the programme being stored in the computer on the machine. It also means tapes can be edited at the machine itself, reducing total tape preparation time and thus increasing utilisation.[15] Going one stage further, CNC has facilitated the development of 'DNC' (direct numerical control) systems, where several machine tools are controlled simultaneously by one central computer. However, while CNC has now virtually replaced NC, DNC is still mainly in the experimental phase, and the cost of these systems is likely to remain prohibitive for the vast majority of engineering concerns for some time to come.

Like other types of automation, NC machinery takes the control of processes – literally – out of the hands of the workers who have traditionally operated them. Rather than being controlled during production proper, the movements of the machinery are now *pre-set*, and the skills involved in machine control are thus effectively 'transferred' to the function of programming.

Programming for NC involves the recording of the specifications of engineering drawings on planning sheets, and their conversion into 'machine-readable' form. At the same time the speeds, feeds, cutting tools required, etc., are also converted. The full programme, normally in the form of a paper or magnetic tape, is then installed in the control panel. Tool setting is done as before, except that decisions on which tools to use are already provided on the programme sheet. Once switched on, the rest is fully automatic.

With conventional NC, any errors in the tape would mean its return to the programming office for modification, and this could mean its travelling to and from the office and the shopfloor several times before production properly got under way. With CNC, however, tapes can be proved at the machine itself – any necessary modifications being made with the first of a batch. The machine's computer automatically stores any modifications in its memory, and at the end of the batch the new, modified programme can be recorded at the machine on a fresh paper or magnetic tape. With some of the very latest CNC systems, the machine's computer memory is in fact powerful enough to record hundreds of programmes, eliminating any need for tape storage.[16]

With machine tools, the control systems are generally introduced as a part of the machinery – the machine supplier doing the 'adding-on'. However, with other applications it is occasionally the case that a new computer control may be added on to existing machinery within the adopting firm, and there are no technical reasons why this method of innovation should not be attempted more often, particularly where firms use highly specialised processes and machinery suppliers are few.

At the same time as machinery on the shopfloor is automated, automatic devices to aid the design and drawing of engineering parts are being introduced in some offices. Working computer aided design (CAD) systems are currently extremely rare in batch production, but again microelectronics, in making them cheaper and more powerful, may make them viable in many engineering firms in the near future. In translating the numerical calculations of designers into actual engineering drawings – either on paper or on visual display units – the traditional role of the draughtsman is likely to be radically changed. It is also possible that programme tapes for production may be produced direct from the same CAD facilities, though viable systems for small batch production are yet to be designed. (In fact, the machine tool manufacturer discussed in chapters seven and eight was devoting some attention to this possibility, but it was not yet a serious proposition.)

Computerised production control is also being introduced into some batch production concerns, but again there are more difficulties than with, say, mass or process production. This is because many engineering shops have an enormous number of small batches of components passing between the various machining functions at any one time. In most shops today, the old manual production control methods which rely on the detailed knowledge of the progress chaser still predominate, but attempts are occasionally being made at computerisation. Our case study of a machine tool manufacturer provides one such instance, and a discussion of both the technical and the social aspects will be found there.[17]

The Effects of Automation in Batch Production

J. Remmerswaal has forecast that the total effects of the technical changes described above will be an increase in productivity of 200–300% by the mid-1990's. Unless demand doubles or trebles (which is highly unlikely) this will mean employment will be reduced by 50% within fifteen years.[18] One must remain highly sceptical of such extravagant claims, though some employment reduction is virtually inevitable. Claims of productivity improvements for *individual* NC machines vary enormously, and much depends on the utilisation achieved. To date, in the UK, it is probable that most labour immediately displaced has been absorbed elsewhere within adopting firms – and certainly this has been the case in most of our case study firms. However, this depends on the expansion – or at least the maintenance – of the firm's market, and displacement effects caused by productivity improvements may only make themselves felt with a change in the economic climate. Thus some of the redundancies being made by our case study firms during the present recession are no doubt due to changes in technology two or three years ago. In this way displacement effects are masked by changes in the fortunes of the firms in the market place, and measurement is made extremely difficult. There can be no doubt, however, that the general trend to reduced employment in the UK engineering industry owes less to automation than to the failure of firms to invest in R&D and new production facilities.[19]

The striving for higher utilisation with automated engineering machinery means that many firms introduce shiftwork and/or increase overtime. Twenty-four hour exploitation of machinery has, of course, been commonplace in many factories for many years, but automation may help increase this trend. Further, white collar workers such as maintenance technicians and programmers are likely to be drawn into the shift system.[20] However, unlike oil refineries and the like where the whole plant is automated and demands twenty-four hour exploitation to be economically viable (and in some cases to be technically feasible), the automation of single multi-purpose machines can be undertaken gradually (i.e., one at a time). It may not be feasible to introduce shifts for, say, two or three machines, and there is thus no simple relation between technical developments and shift patterns.

Our central concern with the changing nature of work associated with the new technology makes exact relationships even more difficult to establish than with labour displacement or shiftwork patterns. However, it is generally agreed that electronic control of production machinery means a reduction in demand for *motor* skills, and an increase in demand for *conceptual* skills. The machine operator may thus lose his traditional role as skilled or semi-skilled worker, and become a machine minder, intervening only when the machine goes wrong, while the new occupation of programmer (or 'process controller', depending on the type of machinery in question) emerges, demanding a whole new set of conceptual skills. At the same time, the new maintenance requirements associated with automation, and in particular with microelectronics, mean that new skills and combinations of skills are required from maintenance personnel.

Probably the best description of real job changes associated with the automation of batch production is that by Erik Christensen,[21] although this work is now out of date. More recent empirical findings are provided by Swords-Isherwood and Senker.[22] (Both studies describe NC technology, but as Christensen himself points out, control systems for other types of batch engineering are very similar.) What both these descriptions have in common, however, is a general failure to establish any clear-cut patterns of work organisation associated with NC technology. Instead they go into some detail on variations established in different factories, both in terms of precise details of design of control systems, and in terms of the working arrangements established with given control systems.

Particularly important for our purposes is the different divisions of labour which were found within different plants, with the demarcation between operator and programmer tasks being blurred, and occasionally the operator even carrying out some programming himself. Similarly, the divisions of tasks between planners and programmers varies – the programmers occasionally by-passing the planners by working straight from engineering drawings. Another variation found was in the setting of the machine's tools. In most cases skilled or semi-skilled machine operators set their own machines, but occasionally a skilled machinist would be responsible for the setting of a group of machines, while unskilled operators simply loaded and unloaded one or more machines.

On the design of control systems, Christensen points out three types – two conventional, and one called 'play-back control', where a skilled operator makes the first of a batch of components while the movements of the machine are recorded on a magnetic drum or punched tape. Play-back control eliminates the need for a specialised programmer, and virtually the only significant difference in operation between this system and a conventional machine tool is that the operator is not required to repeat the same cycle of movements for each of the batch of components. Today play-back control is virtually extinct. Writing later, since the advent of more sophisticated microprocessor-based control systems, Swords-Isherwood and Senker are faced with even more differences in detailed design, and the degree of operator intervention in programming is likely to be different in each case.

The descriptive material of these studies is valuable. Unfortunately however, in both studies an 'innovation' approach to technical change is dominant. Changes in work organisation are presented as the more or less direct result of advances in production technology, which, upon their diffusion, are having 'impacts'. It is the contention of this book that this apolitical approach is inadequate – if not misleading – in explanations of changing work organisation. Before examining the specific implications of the innovation approach for an analysis of the impacts of new technology on *work organisation*, we will briefly outline its *general* assumptions.

The Innovation Approach to New Technology[23]

The innovation approach begins with new ideas and their application: 'An invention, when applied for the first time, is called an innovation'.[24] Attention is focused, in particular, on advances in scientific and technical knowledge, and the way they throw up possible useful applications. If application is successful, and generally this means if found *economically viable*, there begins a process of 'diffusion' of the innovation. Individual firms are forced to 'adopt' the innovation in order to remain competitive (i.e., in order to survive). The diffusion of the innovation then gives 'impacts' which may be intended or unintended, and which may be good or bad. Throughout, new technology is treated as a neutral input to individual production systems, the motivation behind its introduction being purely competitive, and its effects, apart from the improvement of the competitive position of the firm or nation-state, being largely incidental.

Alongside this theory of change, and for the most part barely distinguishable from it, is the literature which is directly applicable, and often is applied, in policy-formulation and decision-making. This literature maps out the conditions for success and failure, and points out how firms, industries, or whole nations, can innovate to maximise competitive advantage. For instance, the conditions under which successful applications (innovations) may arise from scientific and technical research have been explored; if insufficient attention is paid to the market, if investment is too low, or R&D poorly organised, etc., then viable innovations may not be forthcoming.[25] Similarly, the rates of diffusion of innovations are affected by market structure, 'attitudes to change', legal restrictions, etc., which act as 'stimulants' or 'constraints'.[26] And of course, any negative impacts a new technology might have are treated as 'adjustment problems' which must be dealt with if resistance to change is to be avoided. For instance, Mansfield discusses the problem of dealing with displaced labour – often an unfortunate consequence of automation: workers may have to be retrained for new jobs, or even moved to different parts of the country where work is available, etc.[37] Our concern is most centrally with any 'impacts of innovation' at the point of production, and more detailed attention will now be given to the literature which focuses on this aspect.

In the 1960's a series of studies dealt with the effects of automation at the point of production in exactly the manner one would expect in following the logic of the innovation approach. The most famous of these is that by Touraine, published in 1965.[28] The 'adjustment problem' identified lies in the transition from a 'craft' to a 'technical' system of work associated with the introduction of automated production processes. Automation is held to give rise to better physical working conditions, and reduced physical effort, but also to lead to boredom, and to tension from the stochastic nature of the work. It may also disrupt existing workgroup relationships. Resistance may thus be generated, but policies to overcome the resistance – especially in the form of early 'consultation' and 'participation' – may help smooth the implementation of the new technology.

Touraine's analysis and recommendations have since been modified,[29] in particular by emphasising that the transition workers face is less likely to be from a 'craft' to a 'technical' system of work than from an 'unskilled' to a 'technical' system. But the basic concerns remain the same: in order to avoid social and economic distress, and more importantly in order to effectively and speedily implement changes, adjustment techniques must be generated and employed. Both the need for change in the first instance, and the form the change takes, are taken as inevitable consequences of technological advance, and the best choice workers can make is to 'adjust' and 'adapt' themselves to the new working arrangements.

Another set of policy studies which treat work organisation changes as the inevitable result of technological advance are those from the Science Policy Research Unit at Sussex University in the early 1970's. Using the simple deterministic model outlined above, the relationship between technology and skills in the engineering industry were analysed.[30] Assuming that the physical characteristics of the technology determined the skill requirements of firms, they suggested that if the diffusion rates of particular types of technology could be forecast, and the 'skill requirements' of each type assessed, then future changes in training needs arising from changes in technology could also be forecast. Individual firms, and more importantly, national training boards, could then plan more accurately their training programmes with an improved knowledge of future manpower requirements. Management policies within individual firms are treated merely as obstacles to the logical development of the new technology and its associated skill structures, and like the workers in Touraine's study, managers are urged to adapt to the demands of the new technology.

An example of the 'impacts of innovation' approach applied to office technology has recently been provided by Emma Bird in a study of the impact of word processors on female labour.[31] Suffering from the worst problems of the innovation approach, 'information technology' is presented as having 'impacts' on clerical jobs, on equal opportunities, on training requirements, and so on, with little reference to ways in which these impacts may at least be modified by specific organisations.

Apart from these policy-oriented studies, much of the industrial sociology literature has likewise taken advances in production technology as the starting point in analyses of changes in work situations. Whether the focus of interest has been on psychological deprivation (alienation), or shifting skill structures, or industrial relations problems, etc., technology has been taken as a primary, independent, explanatory variable.[32]

The impacts of innovation approach is severely limited to the extent that it treats technology as devoid of its own social and political context.[33] Technology is held to arise somehow from scientific and technical research, and if it so happens to confer competitive advantages then firms must either adapt and accept the consequences – the 'impacts' – or go bust. The *context* in which technical change occurs is treated as of importance only to the extent that it constrains the changes, or is changed itself by the new technology. Thus instead of discussing, for instance, the nature and availability of skilled labour within a firm and the way this might affect the choice and use of technology, the skilled labour is treated simply as a possible constraint (as Touraine points out, craft workers may resist the new technology's demands) *or* as a phenomenon which is transformed by the technology (from craft worker to technical worker). The fact that managers may introduce technology with the *intention of transforming* the nature of work simply will not fit the 'impacts of innovation' framework.

In depoliticising technical change the illusion of a consensus is achieved: it is in everyone's interest that the firm (or country) competes and survives, thus we must adopt the technology and accept its consequences, or else! In this sense the simplistic model of innovation can act as an ideological justification for particular changes which may have *political as well as economic* motivations, and in mystifying the real nature of technology its effect can be powerful. This does not necessarily mean that there can be no consensus at all – for in some senses there clearly is. For example, failure to update production methods *may* mean the firm makes a loss, goes out of business, and causes a good deal of unemployment – at least in the short term. It is this basis in reality that makes the myth of neutrality so dangerous. But it *does* mean that any consensus must be limited, and it is thus one of the major tasks of this book to remove the illusion of consensus in order to display technology as a phenomenon controlled by particular people with particular interests and in particular positions of power. The questions which must be raised are such as 'why does the change take on this particular form?', 'which groups of people instigate the changes?' and 'who are the prime beneficiaries?'

The most important recent work which challenges the neutrality of technology is that of Harry Braverman, and it will now be discussed briefly.

Capitalist Technology and the Working Class

In relating changes in production systems within capitalist societies to the constant attempt to maximise profits (i.e., to maximise the surplus derived from labour), Baran and Sweezy explain the rate and direction of expenditure on R&D, the rate of diffusion of new techniques, etc., in terms of the particular stage of development which capitalism has reached.[34] The 'impacts' of new techniques thus also find their source in the nature of capitalism, and these have been elaborated in Harry Braverman's *Labour and Monopoly Capital*.

Braverman's starting point is the one common to most modern Marxists: when the worker enters into a labour contract, he sells not himself but his 'labour power', and the capitalist is left with the problem of realising the 'full usefulness' of that labour power:

> . . . when he buys labour time, the outcome is far from being either so certain or so definite that it can be reckoned. . . . with precision and in advance. This is merely an expression of the fact that the portion of his capital expended on labour power is the 'variable' portion, which undergoes an increase in the process of production: for him, the question is how great that increase will be.[35]

In other words, no matter how specific the employment contract it remains an open-ended agreement, and its details in terms of work done are finalised only in the day-to-day interactions between workers and their employer (or the employer's agents – managers and supervisors). This translation of 'labour power' into 'labour' is the managerial problem of control identified by Braverman, and in the monopoly capital phase of society's development the solution takes the form of Taylorism and scientific management.

The three important aspects of Taylorism identified by Braverman are as follows: labour is reduced from its craft status to a series of simple tasks (hence the 'homogenisation' of the workers); mental and manual labour are separated (the separation of 'conception' and 'execution'); and the 'scientific' knowledge of the labour process – now completely in management hands – is used to plan in detail, and in advance, the tasks required of each worker. In appropriating the skill and knowledge involved in production, control over the nature and pace of work is placed more directly into management hands, and the advantages for capital are twofold. First, labour is cheapened – an unskilled worker costs less in wages and in training time than a skilled one. Second, and more importantly, the pace and quality of production being in management hands means that managers can more directly dictate the activities of the worker – hence the solution to the problem of the 'variable' character of labour power. Taken to its logical conclusion, the application of scientific management provides 'the ideal toward which management tends':

> The subjective factor of the labour process is removed to a place among its inanimate objective factors. To the materials and instruments of production are added a 'labour force', another 'factor of production', and the process is henceforth carried on by management as the sole subjective element.[36]

The precise means of de-skilling employed by management can take two forms. Capital can achieve its goal either by organisational and disciplinary means (through labour power), or by technological means (through the instruments of labour). Braverman shows how both means are used by managers, and the example of machine tools given by Braverman (fortunately for our purposes) will serve to illustrate what happens.[37] Until recently the skilled machinist remained largely in control of machine shop production. Metal cutting was a craft acquired only by years of experience, and the employer was dependent on the craftsman's own initiative in producing goods of sufficient quality and quantity to make a profit. In Marxist terms, the employer's capital expended on labour power was extremely variable. Thus in order to wrest control of production and to cheapen labour, management set about breaking down the machinist's tasks among machine operators who would work solely on the lathe, the milling machine, the grinding machine, etc., and machine set-up was made a speciality. Operations could then be determined according to Taylorist standards. However, these organisational means of de-skilling met definite limits in the technology, which had to be transformed before further advances in capitalist control could be made. The answer came in the form of numerical control. As explained earlier, with NC the speeds, feeds, movements, etc., of the machine tool can be predetermined in the office by parts programmers who produce a paper or magnetic tape containing 'instructions' for the machine from the planning sheets. Machine set-up is now simply a matter of adding the necessary tools, and when the tape is added to the machine's control cabinet the rest is automatic. By taking advantage of these new processes, management can now ensure that the machine operator is left only with the tasks of pressing the on-off switch, and loading the machinery. According to Braverman: 'He is now definitively relieved of all the decisions, judgement, and knowledge which Taylor attempted to abstract from him by organisational means'.[38] The old skills of the machinist have effectively been transferred to the office.

Thus Braverman's treatment of technology and technical change contrasts sharply with that of the impacts of innovation school, for rather than seeing technology as an exogenous input to productive organisations, it is shown to serve as a functional component in a particular system of domination and control: technology is capitalist technology.

Since Braverman wrote, a number of authors have elaborated his analysis of technology, and applied his arguments in detail to many sectors of the economy. For example Harley Shaiken has examined machine tools in detail, and provides a good deal of empirical evidence,[39] and Mike Cooley, a shop steward with Lucas Aerospace, has written extensively on the de-skilling effects of new technology both in the office and on the shopfloor.[40] A Bravermanesque consideration has recently been given to the application of microelectronics in a range of industries by the Conference of Socialist Economics.[41]

Historical accounts of the development of the 'capitalist labour process' have also been generated, and Stephen Marglin provides a particularly noteworthy argument when he suggests that the factory system itself was the result of capital's attempts to wrest control of the work process.[42] Just as the 'impacts of innovation' school assumes that advances in production technology inevitably represent the most efficient means of production, so most would argue that the factory system replaced the previous 'putting-out' system because it was a less costly method of production. However, Marglin argues that by itself the factory system was *not* technologically superior. Bringing workers together under one roof simply meant that discipline and supervision could be harsher (thus any increase in productivity was explained by a greater *input* – i.e., labour was forced to increase its effort – and not by any inherent advantage conferred by the factory) and also that 'embezzlement' was made very difficult. In sum, what the factory did was to increase profits for the capitalist by extracting more effort and ensuring the gains were fully appropriated by him. It was only later, when innovations specifically aimed at the factory were developed, that any real *technological* advantages over alternative systems came about.

Beyond Braverman

Braverman's thorough critique of managerial practice since the turn of the century has been widely applauded, and is already a classic being quoted by virtually all persuasions of students of industry. It is perhaps ironic, then, that his most vociferous opponents are fellow Marxists. They have presented two very basic problems with his analysis – one is his treatment of labour as an unproblematic and totally acquiescent presence in the labour process, and the other, in some ways related, is the presentation of Taylorism as *the* fundamental practice of twentieth-century management.

Taking the first criticism, that workers are *not* totally compliant to management demands, it has been shown that management attempts to de-skill work have been met by opposition from labour. Braverman, it is held, tends to lose sight of the fact that there is a 'frontier of control', such that workers can play an active part in shaping their own labour process.[43] This often takes the form of unorganised resistance, but on some occasions collective action is more important. For instance it is well known that Taylor himself was opposed by trade unions in the United States. Similarly, skilled workers in the UK engineering industry were able, through collective organisation, to maintain job controls despite attempts to establish new forms of managerial control.[44] (The case studies in this book could be interpreted as an exploration of worker resistance – albeit largely unorganised – in the engineering industry today.) Instead, Braverman presents the workforce as the passive recipients of a de-skilling technology determined by the exigencies of capital accumulation. The domination of labour by capital is presented as virtually complete, and any possibilities for either reform or revolution are treated pessimistically.[45]

Related to this criticism, because worker resistance and/or initiatives may qualify management aims and intentions, many Marxists (as well as managerial theorists) have commented on the possibility of *alternative* management strategies towards the labour process.[46] Special reference has been made to the job enlargement and job enrichment programmes which have been increasingly in evidence in the 1970's. Management strategies are held to be variable over time and in different places, and in the 'humanisation of work' initiatives of late are presented as a refutation of Braverman's universal de-skilling hypothesis.[47] A group responsibility for enlarged tasks and for the finished product is held to be used by management in answer to the lack of cooperation of the workforce due to a disaffection from Tayloristic forms of work. Use of this strategy involves handing back some aspects of control over production to workers, but is held to facilitate managerial control in a more important sense: the *overall* production process remains in the hands of capital, and *ownership* of the means of production remains unchanged.

In summary, by asserting an inevitable and universal impulsion to de-skill on the part of capital and its agents, Braverman presents a vision of work life which is shaped and determined by the historical development of capitalism. In doing so he loses sight (i) of the way workers can, and do, shape their own relationships both to their fellow workers and to the machinery of production, and (ii) of the degree of choice available to managers in their use of technology. Thus any notion of *human choice* or *agency* in technical change disappears behind the logic of an uncontrollable system of capitalism, and in being sceptical of any possibilities of political intervention, Braverman's model tends in its own way to be just as deterministic as that of the innovation school.

Thus while Braverman helps make a nonsense of the idea that technical change has a logic of its own, he fails to show how the direction of change may be *contested* – that is, he fails to show the dynamics of the political processes involved. Instead, he prefers to present change as always and everywhere dominated by the interests of a 'capitalist class', *with no internal dissension and meeting no serious opposition* from other interested parties. The aim of this book is to explore the real political processes at work.

2 The Political Dimension of New Technology

In exploring the politics of the introduction of new technology, it will be useful to consider the contribution of sociologists to the general debate on organisational change, as well as criticisms of technological determinism. Using these two inputs, this chapter will develop our theoretical perspective, and the implications for an examination of the introduction of new technology in batch production will be drawn out.

Technical Change and Social Choice

Traditionally, organisational theory is divided between structural or functionalist approaches, and action approaches. The structuralist approach relates organisational characteristics to size, technology, complexity, etc., while action approaches treat organisational structures as emergent entities dependent on the conscious political decisions of actors and groups of actors.[1]

The innovation approach to technical and social re-organisation is clearly structuralist, in that work organisations are related directly to developments in production technology. Just as other sociologists have treated organisational structures as a function of size of the organisation,[2] the innovation theorists present organisational characteristics as dependent on the technology employed. 'Types' or 'levels' of technology are held to demand particular patterns of work organisation, thus having an independent influence on the experience of work and on aspects of industrial behaviour. A form of economic determinism is the most likely explanation for the development of the types of technology they identify: the technology represents the most efficient method of producing the goods or services offered by the firm. The social impacts are a secondary consideration – the inevitable consequences of technology's own logical development. Thus technical change is depoliticised, and the illusion of a consensus achieved: the firm must compete by introducing the most efficient production techniques, otherwise its survival is threatened.

The central criticism of consensual systems theories, as Tony Elger puts it, is that

> . . . they reify the organisation as an entity with characteristics independent of the social processes through which organisational members construct and construe social reality. The systems theorist assumes that the organisational 'function'. . . . provides an unambiguous and virtually unchallenged referent for action within the organisation, and thus neglects the ways in which actors' purposes and perspectives intervene in the interpretation and contesting of goal-related prescriptions for action.[3]

As chapter one pointed out, for the innovation theorists, actors and groups of actors are important only to the extent that they obstruct or accommodate technical change. For an action approach, they are the starting point. An action approach seeks

> . . . an analysis of the manner in which actors actively and variously interpret and, through the deployment of resources, control social settings within organisations. . . . the impact of organisational goals on organisational action is mediated by processes of interpretation and negotiation in which the various groups of participants attempt to protect and advance their special interests.[4]

Child's use of the concept of 'strategic choice' is particularly useful here. Child urges us to '. . . consider the process of choice . . . in which economic and administrative exigencies are weighed by the actors concerned against the opportunities to operate a structure of their own and/or other organisational members' preferences'.[5] The 'systemic exigencies' which supposedly determine organisational structure can now be seen as *referents* used by organisational members who hold particular assumptions and values, and thus both the pragmatic and moral dimensions of decisions can be taken into account.

With production technology, the immediate objection to this type of view is that as long as firms are in competition, the 'one best way' of producing goods (or services) will inevitably come to dominate as its advantages make themselves felt. That is, the contextual variable of *competition* will in the end always be a determining factor. However, there are at least three reasons to be sceptical of this claim. First, 'productivity' or 'efficiency' cannot be accurately measured, and in any case different interest groups may use different criteria in assessing what is efficient. Second, the total acquiescence of labour can never be assured. Third, even if it could be measured and imposed, there is always more than 'one best way' of designing and using technology. This is not to totally deny the importance of competition and efficiency, but it is to deny their role as sole determinants. Our case studies display how efficiency and productivity may in fact be secondary considerations or, at the most, *constraints on possible options*. We will present a lengthy discussion of the precise role of efficiency arguments in the light of the empirical findings in chapter nine.

Managers and engineers, then, instead of being seen as the intermediaries – the *messengers* – of a technical and economic system which demands they act in accordance with its inherent logic, can now be seen as political beings with particular interests and having particular positions of power. They become the creative mediators between potential and actual technology. They become, and are in fact, responsible for actions which will have very wide effects – economical, technical, political, social, etc. With these, they are able to exercise conscious choices.

The Mediation of Management

In chapter one we used the research from SPRU as an exemplar of the systemic innovation approach to technical change. To be fair, the SPRU researchers have themselves more recently recognised the problems with their analysis:

> . . . it does not seem reasonable to assume that management policies merely delay the impact of technological change on skill structures . . . the 'skill structure' of a particular [. . .] organisation is a function of manpower, training and job design policies, as well as of the economic and technological characteristics of the organisation's activities. . . . future research should be designed to take into account the extent to which both technological change and skill structures are affected significantly by company policies.[6]

Their research, however, has yet to fully abandon the assumptions of the innovation approach. Their most recent work tends to see the particular product, batch size, inspection system, etc., of individual firms as modifying the impact of technology, but the final outcome is still seen simply as that which enhances overall economic efficiency in the circumstances of the particular firm. The importance of social and political motives is played down, and forms of work organisation are still held to reflect the 'one best way' for the set of technical circumstances in question.[7]

In another article referring specifically to computer-controlled machine tools Swords-Isherwood and Senker comment, in a highly ambiguous manner, that with some new control systems managers have the scope '. . . to build in more opportunities for shopfloor intervention to improve performance. Managements may be reluctant to take advantage of this because it would lessen *their* opportunities for controlling output'.[8] This *could* be taken to mean that management control of output will in the long run secure a higher performance. But it is also a suggestion that *issues of control are inextricably bound up with technical change*, and also that *managers have choices to make which are outside the sphere of pure economics*. The case studies in this book are an exploration of exactly these questions, and represent an attempt to uncover the social and political processes which are obscured by previous analyses.

We will show how the technical and social organisation of work can best be seen as an *outcome* which has been chosen and negotiated. Explanations for the variations in work organisation uncovered by empirical studies need not be constantly sought in detailed technical and economic circumstances – important though they may be. Rather, choices in technology and the ways in which it is used can be shown to have a political dimension, derived, as Jeffrey Pfeffer puts it, from the 'contest for control' in the organisation.[9] In this view, the design and choice of technology may be seen as the result of socially-derived decisions, and the way in which technology is used can be explained in terms of the political processes – formal and informal – of negotiation, persuasion, bargaining, and so on.

Political Dimensions of Technical Change

If real choices *are* to be made with regard to technology, then technology must be, at least in principle, a negotiable phenomenon. Various groups within organisations will attempt to impose their own interests on the design and use of technology. As Pfeffer points out:

> . . . if technology is chosen, and chosen using considerations of control as well as efficiency, then it is likely that technology can best be viewed as an outcome, rather than a cause, of fundamental organisational processes. The choice of technology and the organisational design both reflect and affect the distribution of control in the organisation. Each is caused by the contest for control in the organisation, and the resources that are brought to bear in that contest.[10]

There is however, a nagging doubt, because technology, like science, is surely somehow autonomous? – i.e., neutral and value free, devoid of politics. But the objectivity of science itself has recently been challenged, and this includes not only the 'soft' targets of applied social science (cost-benefit analysis, cybernetics, systems analysis, etc.), but also the 'higher' sciences of physics, chemistry and even mathematics.[11] This is not the place to discuss the sociology of scientific knowledge – suffice it to say that the claim that science is objective and therefore divorced from politics is becoming weaker and weaker. As yet there is, unfortunately, no sociology of *technical* knowledge, but our arguments so far have made it clear that technology is politically informed. In particular, production technology and its associated working practices can only be understood by reference to the social actors involved in its design and use. As Seymour Melman summarises: '. . . the shaping of the means of production may be understood as the derived effect of the application of socially preferred design criteria to the properties of materials given by nature'.[12]

Langdon Winner has gone so far as to state that 'technical things have political qualities',[13] citing, for instance, the case of low-hanging overpasses on the highways of Long Island, New York. These, claims

Winner, were deliberately designed and built by Robert Moses – the architect responsible – on the basis of his racial and class prejudices: by discouraging buses, they effectively barred poor people and blacks from Jones' beach – a public park.

In a similar vein, David Noble has attempted to trace the design of computer-controlled machine tools to their social and political origins.[14] Noble shows how in the initial stages of development there were two types of NC system. One, a 'record-playback' system, allowed the machine operator to make the first of a batch of components in the normal way, using the machine's manual controls. The machine's electronic control system would record the movements, feeds, etc., used by the operator; the rest of the batch would then run automatically. The second, what is now conventional NC equipment, involves the preparation of a paper or magnetic tape by programmers, which is then placed in the machine's control cabinet. This leaves the machine operator with the simple tasks of loading and unloading, so that he is effectively deskilled in Bravermanesque fashion. There were no convincing economic arguments in favour of one control system over the other. Rather, the second type was developed out of considerations of control: in the larger firms where NC was first developed and applied, management sought to remove the 'intelligence' involved in production from the shopfloor to the office in order to gain control of production processes from what was considered a problematic workforce. Thus to see the development of NC systems solely in terms of efficiency or the modernisation of equipment is to miss a vital aspect of the history of machine tools.

Within *adopting* organisations, then, constraints on possible work organisations may already have been *inbuilt* during the design process, which could have been carried on largely externally. As Winner puts it, 'artefacts have politics' – machines may embody particular configurations of power and control. In this sense technology *can* have 'impacts' on work organisation and skills. However, adopting firms still have to *choose* technology from available alternatives; the *implementation and debugging* of the technology has yet to be carried on; and new *working practices have to be established* around the new technology. All these processes offer junctures at which actors can (and do) intervene to influence the process of technical change. Technology has no uniform impact, but depends on the social and political intentions of managers and engineers, and also on the way workers respond, adapt and try to influence the outcome. Our case studies are an attempt to map these vital intra-organisational processes.

Research Aims

Previous research has failed to uncover – or even served to conceal – the political aspects of technical change. The tendency has been to treat changes largely in technical and economic terms, and to present any social aspects as dependent variables. Empirical documentation of technical change thus failed to explore the roles of engineers, managers, and workers, except to the extent that they presented 'barriers' or 'obstacles' to innovation, or to the extent that they were changed themselves by the innovation (the 'impacts' of innovation). Where research *has* examined the social forces behind technical change it has tended to explain innovations and their consequences by reference to a social system (normally capitalism) which determines the way technology is developed and is used, without reference to any possibilities for choice in technology and work organisation, or to the negotiation of changes.

In sum, previous research has generally failed to map out the politics of change – the processes of bargaining, negotiation, accommodation, and so on, which we can expect to occur when new technology is chosen and implemented. Thus the major questions which were explored in the case studies were the following:

(i) What are the interests and values of those actors or interest groups who are implicated in the technical change (engineers, managers, groups of workers, etc.)?

(ii) How do they perceive the change and what do they expect to gain or lose from it? Do they intend to impose their own interests during the change, and if so, how? What power resources can they bring to bear on the direction of change?

(iii) At what stage of technical change do interest groups and coalitions attempt to impose their own aims (design, trial, implementation, etc.)?

(iv) Does the technology act, or is it *perceived* to act, as a determinant of, or constraint upon, the form of work organisation which evolves?

(v) How, and through what mechanisms, is technology chosen? How, and through what mechanisms, is the work organisation negotiated? Is collective bargaining or other types of formal negotiation important? Or is the informal negotiation of working practices more important?

The exploration of these processes required the use of intensive observational methods through case studies. Ideally this would consist of sustained participation over the period of each innovation, though of course this was not possible, given that the whole process of change – from design or choice of technology through to the eventual establishment of working practice traditions – could take several years. Thus some 'historical' investigation was inevitable. Again however, a close involvement with the organisation was the best way of securing a knowledge of the ways in which the interests and values of the actors involved impinged on their perceptions of and actions towards new technology.

Interviews with interested parties and the observation of working practices were the most important, though not the sole, sources of data. An outline of research methods, and some comments on methodological problems encountered, can be found in the appendix.

The Case Studies

Before the more detailed case studies were undertaken, twenty seven firms had been visited and at least one manager interviewed from each. These visits provided the basis of a general examination of manufacturing innovation in the West Midlands undertaken by Professor Ernest Braun, Dr. Russell Moseley and myself, and the results have now been published.[15] Some aspects of work organisation from these studies have been described in this book in chapter three, and they provide a background for, and an introduction to, the more detailed case studies.

Being located in the heart of Britain's 'manufacturing base', the University of Aston provided the ideal site from which to conduct empirical research into batch engineering. The West Midlands Region consists of the six counties of Herefordshire, Worcestershire, Warwickshire, Staffordshire and Shropshire, and the new *county* of 'West Midlands'. Most of the case studies undertaken were within the West Midlands county itself, which stretches from Wolverhampton and Dudley in the west to Coventry in the east, and of these, nearly all were within that great urban sprawl on the map which constitutes Birmingham and the black-country.[16]

The West Midlands is characterised by a high concentration of employment in metal processing, and with no ship-building and the heavier industries less in evidence, it represents one of the most specialised industrial regions in Britain. One of the major reasons for the region's specialisation is the strong presence of the motor vehicle industry, which demands a host of firms to provide the components necessary for assembly. Motor vehicle assembly was not included in the case studies, but provided the largest single market for the firms studied.[17]

However, as we shall see below, the original set of twenty seven case studies, for the purpose of this book, served largely as a pilot study to the four more detailed case studies presented. As our focus narrowed to a few specific plants the regional flavour of the project declined, and although they are still exemplars of technical change in the West

Midlands, the regional context is relatively unimportant. Thus claims that they are typical of the region cannot be made. More important is the fact that all the case studies are examples of *innovations based on microelectronics in batch engineering*, and chapter one, accordingly, outlined the specific character of automation in this sector. The case study of events in a machine shop – one of our four major case studies, and by far the most detailed one of those four, taking up two chapters – presents many events which might be familiar to some students of the social aspects of technology, since previous empirical research has been heavily biased towards machine tools. Our other three case studies, however, are from firms in other sections of batch engineering which are relatively unexplored, and although obviously this is not a primary justification for the research, any empirical examination of technical change in these sectors is likely to be valuable.

It may have been more appropriate – if stylistically unacceptable – to place the discussion about the twenty seven case study visits before this chapter on the concerns and aims of the research, since they were an invaluable preliminary to the more detailed studies in two important senses. First, they helped the formulation of research questions, and second, they eliminated the problem of access. Thus in some senses they were used as a pilot study.

Of the twenty seven firms, about a dozen provided good examples of microelectronic applications to manufacturing production processes, and from these, several firms considered suitable for more detailed investigation were chosen. The firms selected were all engaged in batch production,[18] and all provided the opportunity to study microelectronic control devices. Although dissimilar in products and markets, their manufacturing processes were similar enough to make comparisons relevant to the concerns of this study. It was important that each firm provided the opportunity to study the various stages of innovation, and it was necessary that the firms offered access to sufficient individuals or groups of people within the organisation to make examination of political processes feasible.

The twenty seven cases covered the whole range of sizes of firm – in fact from less than ten employees to several thousands. The detailed case studies are of two small firms with around fifty employees each and two medium-sized firms with several hundred. Three of these four firms were divisions of larger corporations, though nonetheless their relatively small size was a notable aspect of the study, since smaller firms are relatively unexplored.

Finally, three notes on style of presentation should be made. Firstly, although written quite soberly and dryly, the case studies are presented as unfolding 'dramas', as in telling a story. The organisation of the empirical material gathered need not have taken this form, but it is hopefully a good way of making a mass of tape recordings and notes intelligible, at the same time making it interesting and readable. More importantly, it should also provide a sense of change and development over time in organisations, rather than give a picture which is static and apparently inevitable. If the reader occasionally sympathises with certain actors or groups, this is all to the good: we are, after all, discussing political events.

Secondly, after some deliberation, it was decided to standardise the English used in quotations from tape recordings. This was not only because a black-country dialect is difficult to write down, but also it could divert attention from some very serious points which were being made.

Thirdly, all firms and actors are presented anonymously for the usual reasons. This is particularly important in a study of this type since some evidence was recorded in confidence. Fortunately, the firms are small enough to make their identification virtually impossible, and thus details have not had to be changed.

3 The Pilot Studies

Technical Change and Reorganisation

Of the original twenty seven firms visited, around twelve had recently applied, or were in the process of applying, electronic devices for the control of their manufacturing processes. This includes four firms who were using NC and/or CNC machine tools, but also other firms who were using sophisticated electronics to control a large range of other manufacturing processes – e.g., electronic controls applied to plating equipment, a forge, die-casting machinery, and rubber moulding machinery. The list of possible applications within engineering, it seems, is endless. This chapter will present briefly the work organisations which had evolved in these firms with regard to this type of new technology.

Only in two cases were the control devices 'added on' within the manufacturing firms. For the rest, the devices came as a part of new machinery. But what all the applications share in common is that in making manufacturing processes automatic, they are taking control of the quantity and quality of production out of the hands (literally) of the workers who operate the machinery. Rather than being controlled during production proper, the movements of the manufacturing machinery can now be *pre-set*, and the 'operator', if needed at all, is really reduced to the level of a machine minder. This does not *necessarily* mean that the operator becomes redundant or de-skilled. Rather, the skills involved are 'transferred' to the pre-setting function, which often means programming, and *someone* has to carry out this new task. But it does mean that manual control of the machine's movements, and thus our conventional idea of 'operator', is eliminated. With many large batch engineering processes, this has in many cases already been achieved through conventional automatic machinery. For example, automatic machine tools are set by the toolsetter (often a specialised task) then the rest is automatic – no one has to control the machine's movements by hand. But for small and medium batch processes, conventional automatic machinery is too inflexible. Electronic controls overcome this inflexibility problem, at the same time as making the production of components faster and more reliable, and often making complex parts both more accurate and more repeatable.

But apart from these more obvious technical advantages, the new technology offers managements the opportunity to reorganise the workforce along new lines. As we shall see, the payment system, shiftworking patterns, manning levels, and in particular the tasks which workers will carry out, are not *determined* by the hardware, but they do have to change. For instance: as described above, process control devices mean that machine operating is a redundant task, and the work of the operator must thus be redefined; manning levels may be brought into question; the payment system may have to change accordingly; and shiftwork may be envisaged as a way of justifying the capital expenditure involved.

Even given the apparent similarity of many of the applications, no clear pattern of work organisation emerged. Rather, a range of organisational intentions and designs were apparent.

Machining[1]

Out of about fourteen firms using machine tools on a significant scale, only four currently utilised NC or CNC. A different approach to dividing the tasks characteristic of this technology was evident in each. At one extreme the tasks of the machine operators were reduced largely to loading and unloading the machines, and to monitoring the process. Programming for the half dozen NC machines was carried out by the managers alone, and this strict task division was justified on the grounds of the complexity of programming (components being produced were highly complex parts for the aerospace industry). The managers claimed they recognised the boredom involved in machine minding, and hoped that future CNC machines, by making programming a simpler task, would facilitate operator programming.[2] In a second case the CNC operators were skilled workers previously familiar with conventional machinery. Here, one or two were becoming involved in programming, but the owner-manager of this small machine shop, perceiving a shortage of skilled labour in the market, talked of using his skilled 'nucleus' in the toolroom on conventional machines, and recruiting unskilled labour to 'mind' the expanding CNC section. In his words, the skill shortage problem '. . . has been forestalled by the introduction of high technology machinery. . . . We *have* to use high technology to expand.' (Recently two 'youngsters' were employed to take on the roles of machine minders.)

Towards the other extreme a third firm had introduced several NC machine tools as part of a large capitalisation programme. The firm had an elaborate personnel policy, which provided extensive training for the setter-operator. Here the setter-operator had the responsibility of making verifications to programmes, but not of actually writing them. In the fourth case all the operators were involved in verifying (or 'proving') programmes to some extent, and some became involved in the actual programming too.[3]

Two other firms were in the process of considering CNC technology, and their intentions were of the two extremes described. In one, a separate department for programming was envisaged – the operators to act as machine minders. In the other, it was hoped that existing setters would carry out their own programming, and some workers had already been sent to possible machine suppliers to examine for themselves the technology of CNC.

In two out of the four cases where NC/CNC was already utilised, shiftworking was used in order to reduce the payback periods of the hardware. But in the other two it was considered that a single-shift system with occasional overtime was adequate. One of the firms using a night shift pointed out that it was desirable that operators were more than mere machine minders if they were to be responsible for production during the night, when there were fewer supervisory and technical staffs. The other was a much smaller machine shop, and managed to run five CNC machines on a night shift with only one person (the foreman) trained to deal with programming problems.

In all cases there was still one man to one machine, and with extra maintenance requirements, plus the new support function of programming, the number of employees per machine rose. However, although precise figures could not be given, output per employee (productivity) rose significantly in all cases due to the higher capacity of the new machines. For instance, in one small machine shop it was claimed that the five new CNC machines provided an equivalent output to fifteen conventional machines. This was typical of the claims placed on NC and CNC, though in no case had this led directly to redundancies – each firm had introduced the new technology during market expansions. However, one could expect them if and when the firm's market declined to the size of pre-CNC days.

No firm used piecework for its NC/CNC operators. Two used a group bonus system, one used average earnings (i.e., a day rate plus what they would normally have earned in piecework payments on conventional machinery) and one used a simple hourly rate.

Thus, although in all cases the new technology was used in similar technical circumstances – i.e., small batches and often for the more complex components – there were a range of possibilities for organising work which were recognised and taken advantage of by managers. These were strongly related to the existing organisational make-up of the firm: for instance, where CNC operators were recruited from the existing skilled labour force, their responsibilities were more likely to be wider; and where unskilled or semi-skilled labour was used managers would have to do their own programming (in the two smaller machine shops) or make more use of specialised staff (in the two larger firms). Similarly, the different shiftworking patterns and payment systems used by the different firms were dependent on the systems which already existed – for instance a firm which was generally committed to high technology and had established shiftworking years ago, tended to use all new equipment on a shift basis, whilst for two firms which had not used shiftwork recently this was not the case, and one of these two had no intention of using shifts in the foreseeable future. The same payment systems tended to continue – the only exception being the case where the temporary use of average earnings in place of piecework was beginning to look permanent.

These strong relations between old and new systems are obviously partly due to the technical need to maintain some continuity and coordination within organisations. The new technology has to 'fit in' with the existing arrangements, especially when introduced slowly over a number of years. Totally separate arrangements are hardly feasible for, say, two or three machines. But one must suspect that they may also be due to certain social and political considerations – in particular, workers are likely to wish to carry on the working practices to which they are accustomed. Thus, for instance, in at least one firm, skilled labour was used to operate CNC machinery in favour of semi-skilled because of union pressure, and in all cases the payment rates on new machines and the system of bonus pay were both the subject of negotiation between managers and unions (or workers' committees).

The direction firms were taking in terms of the organisation of work were dependent on an implicit or explicit strategy which management adopted, and clearly philosophies and strategies varied from firm to firm. This is best displayed by contrasting the two extremes. At one was the owner-manager of the small machine shop who wished to use high technology 'instead of' skilled labour in order to expand. He talked about the 'illiterate and innumerate kids' on the labour market today: 'They're no use to me, so I get CNC instead.' By employing two of these young people as machine minders, and retaining all programming functions for himself and the works manager while the existing skilled workers were used as toolsetters, he was already half way to de-skilling the operators and creating a small elite of highly skilled staff. At the other extreme was the firm with extensive personnel and training policies, where setter-operators were highly trained and responsible for expensive machinery. They were expected to set their own machinery and to assure that programmes were correct – if necessary making changes to the programmes. This arrangement was justified by a director both in terms of increased job satisfaction for the operator *and* in terms of the advantages of having a flexible and responsible workforce. As the director said: 'it pays'. Nonetheless, the work organisation in this firm was no doubt strongly related to a philosophy of, to use management's words, 'participation' and 'delegation of responsibility'.

To summarise, organisational forms characteristic of NC and CNC technology were strongly related to existing forms – partly for technical reasons of continuity and coordination, but also because of political forces deriving from vested interests in existing arrangements. However, the management strategy is not, in the end, determined by these factors, and whatever the real relation between strategy and ideology, managers did perceive their 'philosophy' as playing a central role.

The variety of organisational designs found in machine shops were in many ways similar to those found in other manufacturing concerns where electronic process control devices were being applied, and the mechanisms at work were the same.

Other Batch Manufacturing Processes

As with machine tools, electronic control of other manufacturing machinery eliminates the operator as such, and concentrates the skill in the pre-setting of the process. Again, managements' designs were different in different firms – their organisational intentions ranging from an attempt to 'de-skill' an 'unreliable workforce' with high absenteeism and turnover rates (thus placing control of work in management hands and making labour easily replaceable), to plans to combine several functions (including even maintenance) so that each highly trained 'professional engineer' would be responsible for one machine.

It is particularly interesting to juxtapose these two particular cases, since the first represents a logical response to 'labour problems', and the second also represents a logical response – to *exactly the same* labour problems – high turnover and absenteeism. The two firms are entirely different – the first being a small plating company and the second a large tyre manufacturer, but the particular issue here is the same. The first firm constitutes one of our major case studies (see chapter four) and as we will see, their labour problems were not altogether solved. In the second firm, unfortunately visited only once, there were some unresolved conflicts between various interested groups of employees over who should have control of the new system. When management tries to implement the system whereby a new type of technician takes responsibility – cutting across several traditional job boundaries – one must expect further conflict.

The control implications are quite obvious, and in some cases managers spoke quite openly about 'taking control away from unreliable workers', 'de-skilling the jobs', 'making supervision tighter', and so on. Where the operators' work was *up*graded, managers claimed that 'bringing interest back to the job' would bring the more important benefits of a motivated and reliable workforce.

Even more overtly political control issues, however, were raised by machine monitoring systems. In two cases, machine monitoring devices were being introduced as part of the new electronic control devices. In one case this took the form of a simple digital read-out on how fast die-casting machines were running so that the supervisor could see machine speeds at a glance. The reason was that operators would often run the machines slower than was possible in order to make their work easier. In the other, an elaborate system could communicate to management machine speeds, downtime frequency, and a host of other information. The intention in this case was ostensibly 'to monitor machine performance, rather than the man', so that problems with machines could be rectified quickly. But the distinction was clearly difficult to draw, and management themselves pointed out the likely problems with the 'big brother' aspects, which are expected when the system is implemented.

In several cases managers complained that the transition to the new systems were marked by operators 'carrying over bad habits' and 'still using old ways of working'. In fact in two cases – one on the handling equipment associated with a forge, and one on an automatic plating line – operators would use the manual override in order to manually control what would otherwise be an automatic process. (The same occurrence was found in one of the machine tool firms, and probably existed in others.) These practices, of course, represent a real failure to implement the new technology – old methods are maintained in favour of the new.

Again, shiftworking patterns and payment systems were more a reflection of the existing organisational set up rather than a result of the new methods. For instance all the firms applied their existing payment systems rather than devise and apply new ones to what was often incremental change.

Summary

These case studies show that a variety of organisational forms exists in different firms using very similar manufacturing equipment and techniques, and that the type of work organisation which evolves around new technology is dependent on choices made by management which mediate the 'impacts' of the technology. They also indicate that the management strategy developed necessarily takes into account the existing organisational arrangements – which are in any case partly the result of the same underlying management philosophy. Workers and their representatives were also seen to bring some influence to bear on new patterns of organisation, and one must suspect that, at least at the level of shopfloor interactions, workers negotiate or 'bargain out' detailed working practices.

However, these pilot studies do not show us how the processes of strategy formulation and negotiation really work, and they necessarily fail to take account of all the interest groups involved. That is, they are only 'snapshots' of organisations, from the viewpoint of leading managers. Only longitudinal studies which map developments over time and describe the social processes leading to the establishment of new ways of working can properly explain change. Our more detailed case studies attempt precisely this.

4 The Plating Company

Company Background

The company is concerned solely with plating processes. Zinc, aluminium, chrome, etc. plating are carried out on components mainly of steel. The market has become more unstable very recently, but a deliberate policy of avoiding the motor industry (most components find their way into other consumer goods – refrigerators, washing machines, and so on) has meant there is still no shortage of orders, and the workforce still has as much overtime as it requires. The firm consists of about fifty people, including management.

This privately owned firm was set up in 1964, the owner later passing on the concern to his two sons, who together with a third partner now own and direct the company. Of these three owners, two deal with the technical and production side of the business, and one with the sales and financial side. They employ a works manager who deals with the day to day running of the shopfloor, and a chief maintenance engineer who has a major role in developing, as well as ensuring, the efficient functioning of manufacturing processes. These five people are the management team who between them make all the major decisions of the company.

The workforce consists mainly of unskilled Asian and West Indian labour, many of them women, and there is no union organisation.

The Changes

During 1980 and 1981 the firm changed location to a custom-built factory about a mile from the original site. A move was inevitable – the old premises were decrepit, and both the Health and Safety Inspectorate and the local Council were placing increasing pressure on the firm to move out. Physical working conditions in the old factory could only be described as hellish – in particular, the whole place was wet and cold, there were large holes in the concrete floor where corrosives had eaten it away, and unpleasant fumes filled the air. One of the two brothers who own the place (hereafter referred to as 'the general manager', since this was, effectively, his working role) made a direct connection between these conditions and the high absenteeism and turnover rates. Figures were not readily available, but 'it's commonplace to see three or four leave on Fridays' and absenteeism 'is about ten or fifteen per cent'. The monotonous nature of much of the work was also stated as contributing to this 'problem of unreliability'.

During the move to new premises – that is, when the old plating equipment was being installed in the new plant, two of the plating lines, out of a total of five, were automated. The firm had first experimented with an automated system on one of the lines in 1974, but the technical problem of flexibility held the project up. Changing from one process to another meant going back to the manual stage and resetting, which could take around two hours. Before the flexibility problem was solved the control system supplier went bankrupt, and the project stopped. The new control system supplier was 'chosen more carefully', and this time the system caused few problems. With the new system, changing the process is carried out at the control panel by changing the programme and/or the time settings. This is far easier and quicker, greatly enhancing flexibility. On the last visit (May 1981) the automatic lines had been running for three to four months, and the basic technical problems had been ironed out.

The cost of changing location was around £400,000, and although at the best of times plating processes are not the most pleasant to work with, physical conditions are immeasurably better. However, for our concerns, the importance of the physical improvements lies only in their incidental relation to the interplay between the work organisation and the new control system. The new control system was in comparison a small investment – only £10,000, including programmes. This partly reflects the decreasing costs of sophisticated electronics, but was mainly because the new system was 'added on' to existing equipment.[1] Despite the fact that capital costs were very small, the implications for the organisation of work within the firm were and are very important.

Expectations on Introduction

In this case we can hardly refer to the *workers'* expectations or intentions with regard to the new control system, because only the skilled fitters and electricians were informed of the changes in advance. According to the general manager, the rest 'just get to know', and anyway 'don't really care'. This did not mean, however, that the workforce was totally acquiescent, and we will see below the ways in which they were problematic from management's perspective.

Managers had clear intentions, and before the changes the general manager was unambiguous about the reasons for automation: the firm wished to expand production; a fixed price for the expansion was particularly attractive ('machines don't need wage increases'); and the labour force was 'unreliable' – automation gave the opportunity to expand production without expanding the labour force.

When questioned what jobs would be like on the automated lines, the general manager made it clear that the 'unreliability problem' refers to more than just high turnover and absenteeism. With the manual system, platers (the men who work on the plating lines) had a good deal of control over production – both quantity and quality – and apparently could not be trusted. In particular, platers would often increase plating time – the amount of time components are left in the various solutions – which makes their work easier, but wastes time and plating materials for the management. The works manager was even more forthright, with comments such as 'they can't be trusted', and frequent reference to the notion that some were not very intelligent. Going automatic was to be the answer to these problems too: the platers would no longer control the process, for the control system would be completely in the hands of management: 'We want the operator to just stand there and watch, and stop it if things go wrong.'

We will now describe in some detail the changes which took place, and the extent to which management's expectations have been met in practice.

Design and Implementation

The platers are all men,[2] and there are normally three per line for a total of five lines. On the two lines which have been automated, however, there are only two platers for each line. (The works manager was quick to point out that the two who left did so of their own accord. They were simply not replaced.) Thus even if these lines have only the same output as the old ones, the productivity increase will mean that the new control systems should pay for themselves in less than a year. Exactly how efficient the lines are, and will be in the future, is not known in much more detail than this. The problem is that 'it depends' on so many things, not the least of them being, as we shall see, the way the platers work with the machinery. Thus there is not an automatic increase in productivity and the *size* of the productivity gains is highly problematic.

Apart from this displacement of 'unreliable' labour, the major advantage of the new control system is its use in taking control of the plating process out of the hands of the plater. A brief description of the old process and job tasks will help to make this clearer. On each plating line a set of rails runs along the top of a series of vats containing the various solutions necessary for the plating process. A carriage runs along these rails, dropping and lifting containers or jigs (holding the steel components) into and out of the various solutions in the vats. With the manually-controlled system, after loading up the carriages the plater has to walk alongside (or on some lines, ride with) the carriage, controlling its movements with an attached control lever. Depending on the type of component, the finish required, etc., they are shifted in and out of the various solutions for different amounts of time. On satisfactory completion of these processes the carriages are unloaded, and the process can then be repeated. Thus, platers could easily control the quantity and quality of their work. In the absence of any form of bonus system, management control was largely dependent on close supervision; but no matter how close, the platers maintained a good deal of control, and management's intention with regard to production targets and quality were frequently not met. *Automation*, according to the general manager, should mean that (i) 'unreliable' or 'stupid' workers would now just 'stand and watch' – management should now control the process, and (ii) 'anybody can load and unload and monitor the process – the skill isn't in the platers' hands any more'. Thus high labour turnover should no longer be a problem – 'anybody can do it'.

Computer control of the plating lines means that the movements and timings of the carriages are *pre-set* by feeding the necessary information into the plating line's control panel. Occasionally this involves some programming (carried out mainly by the system supplier, although the chief maintenance engineer is learning quickly) and frequently requires the resetting of the timers. Apart from loading and unloading, the process is then (theoretically) automatic. In explaining how the automatic lines work, the works manager illustrated his discussion with a visit to the shopfloor to see the control panels. Almost unbelievably, this involved walking straight out of the other side of the factory, and into a small building around the back. Here, amongst other electrical equipment, were the control panels. 'The platers can't get at them here,' he said. In effect, the control panels were separated from the plating lines by a wall, as is illustrated in the diagram below. When asked who sets the process controls he smiled and said 'I do'. In fact only three people are allowed to alter the controls. These are the works manager, the general manager, and the chief maintenance engineer. The control panels were placed behind a wall for no other reason than to prevent workers tampering with them, and management have made no secret of the fact that the intention is to wrest control of the plating process out of the hands of a problematic workforce.

We should emphasise here that management could choose the location of the computer controls because they were 'adding on' to their own existing machinery. In effect they could become involved in a design process which might otherwise be carried on away from the factory. In most other firms studied, once a particular machine or piece

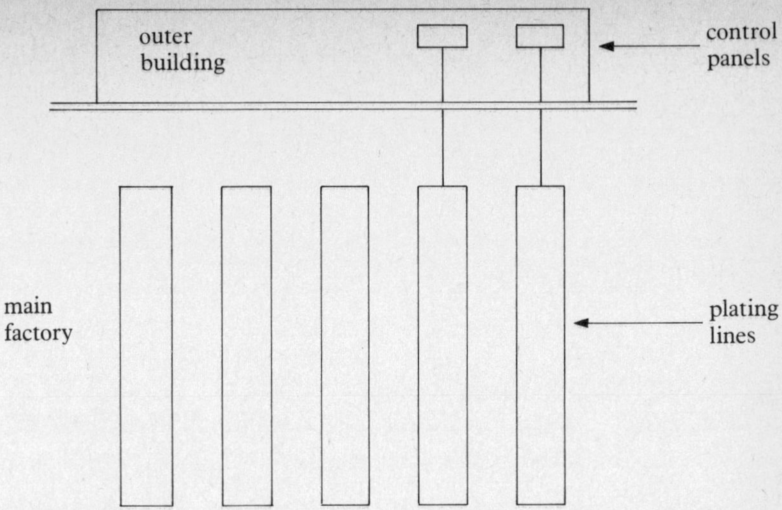

of equipment had been chosen, so had some constraints on the system of control, with very important implications for the organisation of work. Here the firm had attempted to influence the way work would be organised by, in conjunction with the control system supplier, arranging the layout of the equipment in the factory so that the electronic controls for the plating lines would be located in a separate room, access to which was denied to plating line operators. More direct management control over production quality and quantity was thus to be secured by replacing manual controls with electronic ones.

However, the working practices which have emerged have not entirely met management's expectations, and we will now examine in more detail exactly what has happened.

Evolving Working Practices

The works manager, when discussing the reliability of the automatic lines, pointed out that occasionally something goes wrong. For example, components may come out too dull, and the whole batch might have to be scrapped. With the manual system – that is, with the plater in control of carriage movements and timings, he might leave components in the necessary solution for a few seconds longer than prescribed, or return the components to the appropriate vat quickly enough, etc., to rectify any slight deviation in conditions in the vat. But the automatic line, of course, carries on, and not being in control, the plater is far less likely to spot slight deviations, meaning that work may be spoiled.[3] If the plater monitoring the process *is* capable of spotting deviations at an early stage, then corrective action can be taken and the scrap rate significantly reduced. But this is dependent on at least some observational skills. One experienced plater (he had worked on the lines for five years) was quick to point this out, claiming that overall quality of work even on the automatic lines was far better in his hands than in those of less experienced workers.

To cope with these occasional problems the machinery is fitted with a manual override which *is* accessible to workers. Using it is a simple matter of flicking a switch from 'auto' to 'hand', and its occasional use to adjust the programmed process can make the difference between good work and scrap. This is most often the case when new programmes are being adjusted or proved for the first time, and it is thus especially important that platers are involved and motivated during the first few months of automation.

Another example of this stochastic intervention which was particularly important during the first few months of implementation was related by platers. Occasionally a carriage would 'miss' a barrel-full of components and carry 'thin air'. At best the components would remain in a solution for too long a time, and at worse, the carriage would bring another barrel and attempt to lower it into the same vat (which is now empty as far as the computer control is concerned) causing a collision – the result of which could have been extremely dangerous. Here intervention had to be fast and decisive, and fortunately no major accidents occurred.[4] Again, use of the manual override (after, of course, the emergency stop button had been used) saved a good deal of time and trouble.

Although manual intervention has been (and often still is) important to maintain production, the operator's *frequent* use of the manual override contradicts one of management's basic objectives in automation – taking control out of the hands of the workers. Thus the works manager complains that:

> . . . some operators still do not adjust to the automatic lines. They use the manual override if you don't watch them. . . . It's a bad habit. It's difficult to get it into their heads that automatic is the best way. They think they can do a better job manually.

Some of the platers expressed at least some pride in their work, and would frequently use the override to gain exactly the finish they considered constituted 'a good job'. This partly explains their preference for the manual method, with management having problems in convincing platers that the quality of finish they were achieving through manual intervention was higher than necessary, and that the finish achieved by the automatic process was sufficient.

The platers have a reasonable case here, for in 'doing the job properly' they are achieving higher quality and lower scrap rates.

Indeed, *their* idea of 'good work' is given further credibility by reference to the *non-automated* chrome line. Chrome plating is far more 'delicate' – i.e., the work is very susceptible to being spoiled by very slight variations in conditions (for instance, changes in temperatures or strengths of solutions). For this reason, the chrome line is not automated. The process depends on constant monitoring and frequent intervention by experienced platers, and management think it is not possible to eliminate the present *manual* control system. However, management's claim that lower quality and slightly higher scrap rates are tolerable on the zinc and aluminium lines if the potential productivity gains of automation are achieved, is equally logical. Indeed, this *may* make more economic sense than the platers' idea of a good job. But detailed calculations have not been done (and probably could not be done). The impression given is that management may be attempting to justify their political intentions (to gain control over production) by reference to an economic rationale which is far from convincing – and certainly unconvincing to the platers.

Apart from a surprisingly strong sense of pride (given the poor working conditions and the monotonous nature of much of the work) in 'a good job', the other reason why platers would use the manual override was to control the pace of the line. In particular, loading and unloading the lines could become hectic, especially since there are now only two platers per line. A simple flick of the switch from 'auto' to 'hand' gives instant relief from mechanical pacing. Platers can also control pace simply by loading up less carriages, allowing them to carry 'thin air' – though this method is, of course, highly visible. In sum, 'we can slow down a bit when they're not looking', and 'they still come round telling us to hurry up and get the work out'. Thus close supervision is still heavily relied upon.

What seems to have happened is that in being involved in the implementation of the new control system – in particular in having to remedy the mistakes made by the new system until it was 'debugged' by frequent use of the manual override – workers have at the same time been establishing working practices. Now that the technical problems have been ironed out, management feel they are in a position to use the new system as originally intended. However, working practices are now to some extent 'institutionalised', and management are finding great difficulty changing them.[5]

This 'problem', ironically (but predictably) is now compounded by the fact that the vast improvements in physical working conditions with the move to the new factory have meant that labour turnover has virtually ceased. All those now concerned with the new methods have stayed with the company throughout the changes, and there are no signs that they may leave in the future.[6] Thus ironically, management's 'unreliable' workforce have suddenly, in one sense at least, become reliable – i.e., they turn up every day. However, they are still considered unreliable in the sense that they 'cannot be trusted', leaving managers in the unsatisfactory position of having a workforce still in control of quality and pace of production.

5 The Optical Company

Company Background

This optical company is concerned mainly with the manufacture of lenses and the making of spectacles to prescription (a prescription comes from the optician, and a pair of spectacles is returned from the factory to the practice). About 1,600 to 2,000 pairs per week are produced. A small but expanding section of the company is the Instrument Division, which designs and manufactures industrial profile projectors for inspection functions in a range of industries. This section, however, has only two or three employees, and will not be a concern of this case study. Recently the recession has begun to affect even this company, and although the slight drop in sales is unlikely to seriously damage the firm in any way, its expected expansion will now be delayed for the foreseeable future.

The company belongs to a group of companies which altogether employ about 350 people, with total sales of around £4m. The optical company itself employs 45, and its own sales are about £1m. The group includes a chain of Midlands optical practices, and although the optical company is closely connected to them, a customer–supplier relationship is maintained. Operating very autonomously from the group – the directors rarely being seen even by the general manager – there is a good deal of room for internal manipulation. A capital sanction scheme is operated by the group, but 'once the capital is approved, we can swap and change our investments'.

Including foremen, the internal management team consists of seven people, and is represented in the diagram on page 42.

The Changes

Since 1978 the whole factory has been rationalised, reorganised, and modernised – under the direction of a new general manager who was appointed just prior to that by the group main board. Before his arrival all production was in one room, which he described as 'a maze'. The

- group main board
  - managing director (also on board)
    - general manager
      - manager (instrument division)
      - production manager (spectacle production)
        - metal glazing supervisor
        - plastic lens glazing supervisor
        - surfacing section supervisor
      - commercial manager (buying)

surfacing and glazing sections were segregated, production 'lines' were straightened up, and a computing room was created. At the same time the general manager set up the system for the collection of data on internal trends – rejection rates, maintenance requirements for machinery, and so on – so that remedial action could be taken on more easily identified problems and bottlenecks. Also, the group bonus system was reorganised so that workers could understand its mechanics more easily, and so that bonus pay was related more directly to output.

The most interesting changes for our purposes are the new pieces of machinery and equipment which have been introduced over the last few years. The firm now prides itself as 'one of the most advanced producers of spectacles in the UK'.

New Equipment

In the surfacing section[1] the firm has for some time used automatic machinery – rather than hand controlled machinery – whereby the machine is set, switched on, and the rest is automatic. (Hand controlled machinery still has to be used for some jobs.) The task of setting has recently been simplified through the introduction of a computer. Previously a skilled worker would receive a prescription for the lens to be made from the optician (every lens is unique) and from this would make 'rule of thumb' guesses as to which blank to use, and which tools and settings to apply. Before being made perfect, the lens may have to be 'recut' several times – surfacers would tend to underestimate their initial calculations because more can always be taken off the lens, but not put back on. Blank selection, tool selection, and machine settings can now, however, be predetermined by use of a computer, which is programmed to translate that information into which machine settings, etc., to use.[2] The woman who does this 'computing' sends the information from the computer room upstairs to the surfacing room. The surfacers can then simply follow the instructions on the ticket to select tools and set up machines. An accurate lens is then produced in one cut, meaning faster production runs; and the elimination of guesswork means a far lower scrap rate.

The de-skilling implications of the new methods are their most important feature, and these will be discussed below. However, it is worth mentioning the implications for the group bonus scheme. The surfacers' bonus pay is separate from that of the rest of the factory – their bonus being related to the number of lenses they turn out each week as a group. Traditionally, through varying their effort, they have been able to control between them the amount of work they turned out, and thus their bonus. But now, especially with the current slight shortage of work, the amount they can do depends on the amount of lenses 'computed' by the woman downstairs, and sent up by her to the surfacing room. Control of bonus pay by surfacers is now dependent on her cooperation, and so far this has been forthcoming – the surfacing section supervisor himself carrying out the necessary liaison.

In the glazing section[3] the firm has over the last few years introduced a variety of automatic equipment. This includes automatic edging machines – which shape the lens to fit the frame, and put the 'V' on the lens which allows it to be held by the frame; and electronic focimeters – which make the task of lining up the lens for an accurate fit in the frame far simpler. There is a small production line in the glazing section, and the various tasks involved are rationally segregated.

Taken together, the new machinery and the division of labour on production line principles take a good deal of the skill out of the work, and this aspect of innovation for both surfacing and glazing sections will now be discussed.

De-skilling

The firm's policy towards production machinery is to buy the best and the most modern. The general manager and the production manager make the choices of particular machines and pieces of equipment, spending a good deal of time visiting exhibitions in Europe to ensure that they are up to date with the latest. They try to replace most machinery 'every five years' in any case, and as innovative machinery comes on the market they buy it.

The de-skilling which most of this modern equipment entails is seen as an unfortunate side effect which management themselves would not have chosen. The production manager and the metal glazing supervisor are particularly articulate on this matter, both having been in the business most of their lives, and both still considering themselves to be craftsmen. They talk about the change from highly skilled craftsmen to semi-skilled machine operators, and this transformation is perhaps most clearly seen in the case of surfacing, where the surfacer's work is largely reduced to carrying out instructions on a ticket which comes from a computer. The extent of the de-skilling is perhaps best displayed by reference to the new surfacing supervisor, who is in fact a master glazer. He has been in the surfacing section for several months only, but by working to computer print-outs his work is as good as anyone's, and he is quite capable of supervising the section.

The lens computing, on the other hand, involves about six months in training and experience to be carried out competently (surfacing section supervisor's estimate), and thus hardly represents a real 'transfer of skill'. In fact, the skills involved in surfacing have now been *divided* between first, the surfacing machine setting and operating; second, the computing; and finally the programme writing, which has now been largely completed by a consultant, in conjunction with the production manager, although improvements to the programmes are occasionally added, and constantly sought.

The typical attitude of the experienced surfacers to the new machinery, according to their supervisor, is that they 'admire the new machinery, but prefer to work with the old'. The supervisor also comments that surfacers, during the transition period, would always blame any faults in finished work on the computer. Now, the computer is trusted and accepted as reliable, and tooling is the first thing to be examined when anything goes wrong.

In the glazing section a small conveyor transports the spectacles from work station to work station, and workers carry out fragmented tasks as the work reaches them. The lenses are prepared for glazing by being lined up on focimeters, then ground at the edges on edging machines. Both 'lining up' and 'edging' are becoming simpler tasks with the latest machinery. The firm currently has a microelectronic focimeter on trial, which in effect 'reads' the lens by laser beam and does its own calculations: 'there's no training needed to operate this', according to one supervisor. The edging machines are automatic, working from plastic lens shapes – i.e., depending on the shape of the frame, a plastic replica of the shape required is fitted into the machine, which then follows its contours to grind the lens to fit the frame. Operating these machines is simple enough as it is, but the firm is now considering the latest advancement, which is a microelectronic device capable of 'memorising' thousands of lens shapes. When added to the automatic machines, the operator would simply punch in the appropriate number, and the rest would be automatic. Apart from eliminating plastic lens selection, the cutting of new plastic replicas would be virtually eliminated, since the memory store is enormous and recall is instant.

Moving down the line, lenses are next 'rammed in' to the frames, before being rechecked and finely adjusted, using once again a focimeter. In this section, therefore, both new machinery and a fine division of labour based on that machinery (i.e., there are focimeter operators, edging machine operators, etc.) means de-skilled work for the glazers.

Given all this 'de-skilling' (to use management's own phrase) one might have expected the managers to attempt to take advantage of the *control* possibilities. That is, the quality and quantity of production could have been controlled directly by management, rather than relying on the judgement, skill and discretion of the workforce. In particular, skills could easily have been concentrated in the hands of a very small elite of technicians, and operators transformed into unskilled, cheaper, and replaceable labour. But this was not the course taken, as we shall see below. Further, the pace of production could have been controlled in far more *direct* ways than through a simple group bonus system based on output. There are obvious ways in which a production line's pace can be controlled, but neither mechanical pacing nor machine monitoring have been considered as possibilities. Effort was judged solely on final output, and the pace of work determined quite informally by workers themselves. (In fact what tended to happen was that towards the end of each week, production figures were considered and the bonus possibilities weighed up. By working at a steady pace, or by going faster, the workers could to some extent control the amount of bonus achieved.) Similarly, one might have expected management to take advantage of the new strategic position of the computing function in relation to the output of the surfacers. In fact, consideration was given to the idea of persuading surfacers to do some of their own computing, and even of installing computing facilities in the surfacing room itself.

Job Rotation

The general manager and his supervisors talk enthusiastically about the technical advantages of the new machinery, and spend a good deal of time keeping up with the latest developments in Europe. As we have already mentioned, the production manager as well as the general manager try to visit other companies in Europe, and often travel to the exhibitions. In fact to hear them talk, one suspects the interest to be as much a hobby as a simple concern to improve the company's efficiency.[4] But they are unhappy about the effects the new machinery has on the workforce. For instance, after describing at length what a 'remarkable device' the new focimeter was, the production manager complained that:

> . . . there's no training needed to operate this, so it's de-skilling the job and I don't like that, I like to train somebody . . . All you need to know is about four different movements, whereas on a focimeter [of the old type] you have to know what you're doing – you have to know the plus and minus aspects of the lenses.

It was the general manager, however, who was responsible for actually introducing a system of job rotation. Arriving only three or four years ago, and bringing with him a strong philosophy of participation and involvement, he has now managed to establish job rotation as an institutionalised (and compulsory) practice, so that workers now rotate automatically and regularly from job to job, and so that any new recruits are given training in a range of functions. Job rotation is not generally practised *between* surfacing and glazing sections – only within them. This is mainly because surfacers have wished to hang on to their traditional position within the firm: most of the surfacers are long-serving and highly skilled in their craft, and would object to job changes between sections.

We should also mention that not only the most de-skilled of the jobs were rotated. The placing of a glazer in charge of the surfacing room is an obvious example; and as this same glazer (now surfacing supervisor) pointed out, the person carrying out computing, after several months training had made her proficient, was likely to be 'moved on' shortly: '. . . she's very good at her job now – which indicates that she'll be moved soon'.

The immediate psychological advantages of rotation are obvious: '. . . the staff like it, they like the change. Because there's some boring jobs out there!' But job rotation is connected by the management also to a set of advantages which are economic to the firm. In particular, rotation means that absences due to sickness or to holiday can easily be covered. As the production manager pointed out:

> . . . when the holiday season comes on, and I say to a girl, 'Look, you come here and work that machine', we're OK . . . the staff are now reaching a point where I can move them around anywhere I want – and that is a wonderful thing for a production manager to say.

Similarly, a multi-skilled workforce means that shifts can be used with a minimum of supervision. A two-shift system is a possibility for the future, and the general manager considers that this advanced preparation is vital.

Also, the psychological advantages themselves were pointed out as having direct economic advantages in terms of increasing motivation and involvement in work, thus decreasing the possibility of errors (which can be more costly on expensive machinery) due to inattentiveness.

Alongside the rotation of jobs was a policy of careful personnel selection – at least a 'certain level of competence' was required – and this not only ensured a minimum capability, but provided possibilities for promotion to supervisory jobs in the future. Four of the recent recruits were in fact undertaking apprenticeships, and the expense involved for a firm as small as this is perhaps the best evidence of the firm's determination to maintain and utilise a skilled and flexible workforce, rather than a set of specialised, de-skilled machine minders.

Comparing this firm with the plating company displays the folly in the notion that de-skilling and increased management control over production processes necessarily lead to increases in efficiency.[5] In this case the return of control *to the workers* ensured a more effective productive unit. The irony is that managers in the plating company, via their involvement in the design of the new system of production, had the opportunity to build *into the technical system itself* more interesting and responsible jobs. The optical company had to settle for the amelioration of the effects of a given (i.e., externally designed) technology.

To summarise, we might characterise the firm as being the recipients of a Tayloristic technology designed to de-skill what is traditionally a craftsman's domain. To alleviate the worst psychological effects, and to ensure a responsible and flexible workforce, the management have introduced an extensive and very serious system of job rotation. This does not mean that craft skills are retained – on the contrary, the tasks involved are very different and the processes are more resembling 'a science rather than a black art'. But it does mean a very different way of working than would otherwise be the case, and this is reflected in the large amount of time and attention paid to training. The importance of the firm's management, then, in shaping the social and technical organisation of work around the latest spectacle producing machinery, should not be underestimated.

6 The Rubber Moulding Company

Company Background

The main manufacturing process of the division concerned is precision moulding of medium to large batches of rubber components, and about 80% of total output goes either directly or indirectly to the automotive industry. In 1974 there were 650 employees, but since then, through rationalisation and the updating of manufacturing techniques, numbers have been reduced to as few as 350 employees, even though output is now slightly higher.[1]

The group to which the company belongs is a large one, employing several thousand in all. However, the company does operate fairly autonomously from the larger group in terms of internal organisation and decision-making. For major technical decisions the technical manager and general manager appraise the possibilities, and forward proposals for sanction by the group.

The Technical Changes

In 1975 two major new projects were embarked upon by the firm. Both were internally generated, and according to the technical manager they were to enable the firm to remain competitive – improved quality and cheapness being the primary considerations.

The first was injection moulding, to make components previously made on steam presses. The new injection moulding process vastly increases productivity, through increasing the number of parts produced per mould, and more importantly through reducing cycle times (the previous cycle included twenty minutes just for the rubber to become vulcanised; the new time is less than two minutes).

The second was flashless moulding – a new method of transfer moulding. Again the number of parts per mould is increased, and in this case an advantage is that there is virtually no process waste.

Both processes are electronically controlled (the control devices are solid state), and it is the new requirement of setting and adjustment of electronic control devices, along with the new maintenance needs, which have the most important implications for the reorganisation of work.[2]

Expectations on Introduction

The first of the changes was injection moulding, and the new injection units were gradually introduced straight onto the shopfloor from the machine manufacturers. Supervisors and operatives were slowly introduced to the new machinery, which was placed in a partitioned-off pen in the middle of the production area. Flashless moulding was introduced in a similar manner.

Management intentions with regard to tasks were to separate more completely the labour involved in (i) setting and adjusting machinery, and (ii) operating machinery between process control and operating functions. The process control department was expanded to meet this desire, and training needs became far more complex with far more parameters to control, and faster cycles necessitating more precision. Supervisors and maintenance workers (mechanical and electrical) needed extra training to cope with the new processes, and this was done in conjunction with the machine suppliers. For operators, however, according to the senior process controller: 'it's just training for a different mechanical task'. No special training was given, apart from on-the-job teaching.

With regard to payment and effort, management intended to maintain the existing piecework system – the piecework part of the wages providing a significant amount of the operatives' pay, and (theoretically at least) the degree of effort critically affecting this portion.

The strongest explicit concern of workers and their representatives during introduction was that operators who were currently employed should be given the opportunity to man the new units. Mainly because the new work was far less strenuous, the union did not want outsiders taking the new work. As a shop steward put it:

> . . . when these presses were implemented [. . .] we didn't want new labour on there; we wanted existing operators, to give them a chance to come off the heavy job onto the lighter job. These, flashless and injection, they're a lot lighter work – it's nearly all press buttons, whereas we'd been working on the loose moulding, the heavy stuff, say ten, fifteen years. . . . Which I think is only common sense really – people have been working for ten years on a heavy job and a new piece of machinery comes in where you've only got to press a button; you want your blokes to work that machine don't you – pressing a button instead of throwing moulds about. And that's the way we worked it. The blokes off the old heavy jobs first and *then* bring new labour in. In fact, every person now working on injection and flashless has worked on the . . . heavy moulds.

Alongside this concern to keep the work 'within the family', the workers saw that the new moulding units produce more parts far more quickly, and at less cost. Thus, as the manufacturing manager informed me: '. . . the firm was not only using its most expensive labour in the loose moulders . . . but was also facing demands for a slice of the cake'.

In sum, sources of manpower, the division of labour, and payment and effort were the major contentious issues on the initiation of the project. (Both the manufacturing manager and the technical manager pointed out that prior to its introduction the concept of automation and the reasons for it – 'to compete and survive the company must utilise the most efficient techniques' – were explained to the workforce. Both were keen to note that there was never any dispute over the basic principles.) As we shall see, during ensuing negotiations the three issues became inextricably intertwined, and it would be inadequate, if not misleading, to describe the developments as if aspects of work organisation existed independently.[3]

'Productionisation'[4]

Over the next couple of years the new processes were established within the firm, and not until the end of 1977 for injection moulding, and the end of 1978 for flashless moulding, were agreements with the unions over payment schemes and systems of operation finally thrashed out.[5]

In both cases the machinery was introduced straight from the supplier to the shopfloor, and before anything like full-scale production could be set up some development and adjustment to accommodate the firm's particular needs had to take place. Management's first problem arose almost immediately. In the manufacturing manager's own words: 'Development in the production environment meant that the operator would productionise machinery, and rather than management giving production parameters to the operators, the operators would to some extent give them to management.' That is, workers became very familiar with the units, performing wider functions than was expected of them – for example some routine maintenance and process control setting. Management would have preferred process control and development staffs to establish the processes. They suggested that 'green labour' would have learned the limited and specialised tasks more quickly, not carrying over 'bad habits'.[6] Also, productionisation would have been left to the appropriate personnel had new labour been recruited. In fact what happened was that with injection moulding management agreed with unions that people in the old loose moulding areas should be given the chance, in order of seniority (i.e., in order of length of service with the firm), to work with the new machinery. When flashless moulding came along management were 'aware of the problem', but had little choice but to recruit labour on the same grounds.

However, the major problem which management found, and the one which took up most time in subsequent formal negotiations, was that of re-establishing piecework rates on the new machinery. Operators might be persuaded to call in the process controller rather than tamper with the settings, but payment and effort were central and legitimate union concerns. This does not mean that the other problems mentioned above were necessarily peripheral ones. Rather, those areas tended to be subsumed under the problem of the payment–effort bargain. As we shall see, the issues were inextricably linked.

On introducing the machinery, piecework payment would obviously not be possible until technical problems had been ironed out and employees become familiar with the new processes. Thus, regardless of effort, during this phase operators were paid average earnings (the amount they had earned in previous months in the old press shop). At the same time operators were becoming very familiar – if not technically competent – with the processes.

About six months after the introduction of the first injection unit management decided the time was ripe to introduce piecework. However, operators were enjoying average earnings and resisted this move. Another twelve months passed before an agreement was reached. Management eventually 'bought out' the operatives' average earnings by slightly raising, and backdating, the standard hourly payment – to be paid in a lump sum. For the piecework portion of pay, it was agreed that the new technology should yield an earnings potential equivalent to that on loose moulding. However, with the mechanics of the payment–effort bargain at last established, the work study engineers still had to put prices on individual jobs. Here, because of their involvement in productionisation, operators found that they were in a favourable position to use the various technical 'hiccups', etc., to justify higher rates than the time-study man would normally allow. Today – a couple of years later – the chief work study engineer feels that 'fair' rates have now been established:

> Certainly now, the things that an operator can do to beat the system if you like, are generally now known. . . . So I think we now know far more readily the sort of things that they can do. We either then accept that – we'll still pay for that – or we change the method of operation if it's something that has changed on the process. . . . So, on that sort of thing it's generally brought to light now far more readily.

But these problems were enough for management to have 'learned our lessons': in future productionisation will be carried out away from the shopfloor.

Emergent Work Organisation

Probably the most striking change in work organisation is the substantial transfer of skill from the shopfloor to the office. In particular, although shopfloor operatives had always been classified as semi-skilled, the more experienced workers and the foremen in the loose moulding area previously played a major role in setting and adjusting machinery. Now it is *more or less* established that setting is carried out by process controllers. The senior process controller commented: 'They [operators and foremen] like to have a twiddle. The only control we don't mind them adjusting to a minor degree is the injection pressure control.[7] Apart from that we like them to leave it alone.' In fact, operators never fully developed a desire to set and adjust machinery. They were convinced (rightly or wrongly) that it was beyond their capabilities. A supervisor told me: '. . . process control – they're experts at that kind of thing . . . they decide all the settings, the timings, the cure times and everything. Our chaps couldn't do that, well, *I* couldn't do that.' The impression given was that this issue was channelled into the overriding concern with payment and effort, the question of who controls the immediate work process being treated mainly as *incidentally* important. The question of why this group of workers had such an overriding concern with pay is very important, particularly since otherwise negotiations could have taken an entirely different direction. Some clues may come from the facts that (i) operators were recruited according to *length of service* from existing semi-skilled piecework areas – thus they were highly familiar with, and perhaps even resigned to, an instrumental approach to work; and (ii) management never encouraged the development of other expectations to do with work satisfaction or skill enhancement. Perhaps it is hardly surprising that concerns other than pay were never properly developed.

All the same, divergences from a *strict* division of labour *do* occur frequently, and as with the above 'twiddling', they are encouraged by management when a slight deviation from the rules will help production along, and sought by workers when they might increase piecework payments. Occasionally both managers and workers feel they gain from this. The chief work study engineer provides an example:

> . . . in the flashless . . . we have knowingly allowed for operators to go around the back of the machine, every cycle, to open the guard at the back and ensure that the surface – the undersurface of the pattern – is clean. Sometimes you get pips sticking in. We have purposely allowed that in the system, and we pay them on every cycle based on an average that we measured during extensive studying. We *now* know that that does not apply on every cycle – so they can gain a few seconds on every cycle by not going around. They might go around now once in every five cycles instead of every cycle. But we still allow that frequency of one in one . . .

Workers will also, of course, use any other means to beat the system. For instance the Work Study Department is currently keeping a close watch on the amount of time booked as 'waiting time': 'Operators are booking waiting time while still running the presses. The less time booked on the job, the higher the performance.' However, overall the possibilities for beating the system have been greatly reduced: '. . . that opportunity has been reduced on the new technology . . . because the jobs are of a more repetitive nature and you know what is likely to happen. Older processes, it was more of an operator's individual ability to overcome certain problems which obviously meant everybody learned.' And as a supervisor said:

> On injection . . . being governed by the machine we can tell how many heats they can do a day – what's the maximum performance they can do. . . . In loose moulding they could [go above that performance] because, as I say, the faster they go, the more they can do. If they had breakdowns they could do so many heats and put a waiting card in – say for about three hours – and you're getting cards in with a two hundred performance or something like that! And you could argue and argue but you couldn't prove that they couldn't do it. But on the electric machines you know exactly the amount they can do. There's no way they can overbook.

(In fact workers still do overbook according to the chief work study engineer. But this overbooking can now be done only up to a *known maximum* performance.)

We should also note that when agreements on the new technology were finally reached, the union negotiators managed to gain a 16% relaxation allowance. Again, because operators were involved in productionisation they were familiar enough with the machinery and its problems in operation to negotiate a higher rate than might otherwise have been the case. Today there is a continuing argument over interpretation of the allowance. Instead of using the resting time intermittently, as management intended, many workers will work at full pace for most of the shift, and then relax for the last hour or two.

Lessons Learned by Management, and the New Development Area

Although management expressed no dissatisfaction with the *eventual* outcome of the changes, they saw enough problems in 'productionising' on the shopfloor to convince them that a separate development area was vital for any new projects. This has now been built, and three major new processes are being developed within it. Unfortunately they are at the moment confidential (to keep the information out of the hands of competitors) so we cannot go into detail, but the expectations with regard to work organisation were made clear by the manufacturing manager. Productionising away from the shopfloor means that the establishment of working practices and of piecework values will be far less problematic. As soon as the new machinery comes into the hands of the production function full-scale production will be immediately possible, and negotiations straightforward: '. . . once you've negotiated and established a time it's a hell of a job to change that'.

Already the production managers feel they have benefited from the new development area, since new moulds for new components are now developed here. Thus each time the product changes, operators do not any longer have the same chance to use their own preferred work methods. These are already established in the development area before the new work comes onto the shopfloor. But through pressure of getting work out to customers the theoretical benefits are not always realised. According to the chief work study engineer:

> . . . jobs will go out to the production shop in a condition we cannot put a piecework time on – it's not consistent . . . and that ends up then with us paying an average earnings form of payment to operators, and obviously operators, they want piecework really. . . . But after a few weeks of average earnings they don't want to go back onto piecework. There's a little bit of resistance . . .

Exactly what happens when the new processes are introduced is yet to be seen. The important point here is that through their experience, management have come to see the new means of productionisation as their way of taking this phase of technical change outside the sphere of influence of machine operatives. Managers have recognised 'productionisation' as a vital juncture at which the interests of strategic groups can become incorporated into the technical and social organisation of work. They are trying to make sure that the interests built in are their own.

In effect, a *management bias* has been *built in* to the physical organisation of the factory, and we have a clear case of social choice in factory design. As Langdon Winner would put it, *artefacts do have politics*.

7 The Machine Tool Manufacturer – Machine Tools

Company Background

The company is a major machine tool manufacturer located in the West Midlands. It changed hands in the mid-1960's, and again in the mid-1970's. In the summer of 1980 the firm was taken over by an American-based transnational corporation. The first research visit was just before US involvement, the bulk of the research being carried out in the autumn of 1980 and the first few months of 1981.

In the 1950's there were over 2,000 employees at this site, but since the late 1960's the figure has been less than 1,000. With the impact of the current recession, numbers have fallen from around 650 in April 1980 to 550 in October, and down again to around 450 in May 1981. The latest redundancies came after a three day week had been worked by most sections of the shop for around six months.[1] The manual worker to staff ratio is 1.85:1, and of the manual workers almost 70% are recognised as 'skilled', about 20% 'semi-skilled' and 5% 'unskilled'. There are about twenty apprentices. There can be little doubt that the formal 'skill structure' of the manual workforce is partly the result of trade union preferences,[2] but certainly there is a high proportion of very highly skilled manual workers.

The firm produces a range of conventional and computer-controlled machine tools, many for export, and most to customer specification. Production is mainly in small batches, and the major operations are casting and heat treatment, machining, and assembly.

The US parent company have so far left the internal management structure intact, and for manufacturing innovations today the central figure is the manufacturing director, who actively involves himself in all aspects of technical changes. Together with the managing director he makes the major investment decisions, although as we shall see many other actors are very important.

Representatives of the American firm have visited the plant on several occasions, but mainly at boardroom level. Any influence on internal organisation for manufacturing will thus be through the manufacturing director, and it is difficult to determine exactly which aspects of managerial policy and strategy come from the American firm, and which from the internal directors. However, one may expect that the US corporation will generally seek a radical rationalisation. Certainly managers inside the British firm expressed this expectation, and according to a recent article in the *Financial Times*: 'More products from an unchanged or smaller workforce is a recipe which [the American corporation] has successfully applied to a long series of acquisitions within the US'.

Chapter one pointed out the types of technology characteristically being introduced in many machine shops today. This firm provided the opportunity to study two of them – computer numerical control of machine tools (CNC), and computerised production control. CNC is the subject of this chapter, and the changes in production control make up chapter eight. Both provided excellent insights into the ways in which social and political considerations come to be 'built in' to aspects of the technical organisation of the firm. The computerisation of the production control system presents something of a slight digression in that it is not, like the other case studies, the automation of a physical production process. However it is a central problematic activity to all batch production firms, and its study allows us, as we shall see in chapter eight, to gain a more complete picture of the work organisation in our major case study firm.

Computer Numerical Control of Machine Tools[3]

Before beginning our discussion of CNC we should mention the previous use of *NC*. There are five NC machines in the factory, though their designs are now quite out of date. For various technical reasons they never became dominant, and have in any case now been superseded by CNC machines, which are far more appropriate to the small batches characteristic of this plant. Of these five machines, only three are used *as* NC. On the other two the operators virtually always use the manual override to use them as conventional machines – a precedent worth bearing in mind when we discuss working practices on CNC.

The first CNC machine tools for use in production were introduced only four years ago – even though the firm had been manufacturing CNC machinery for over ten years. Today nine CNC machines are being used, and there are plans to introduce more in the near future. As we have seen, the technical and economic advantages of NC and CNC machinery over conventional machine tools are potentially very substantial, and the firm's adoption of computer control should obviously be understood in this light. However, the exact type of equipment chosen and the way in which it was and is utilised is dependent on certain social and political considerations. We shall concentrate on these.

Since the first CNC machines were introduced there has been a change in the senior management team (an important point, the significance of which we shall see later) and thus it is difficult to talk in detail about motivations for the choices of particular machines. The way choices are *now* being justified *can* be examined, but a discussion of choice of hardware will be left until after a description of the evolution of current working practices, since these are now taken into account in decision-making on new technology.

Eight out of the nine CNC machines currently utilised were designed with the intention that programming should be carried out away from the shopfloor – the result of the programmer's work in the office being a paper tape which, when installed in the machine's control cabinet, directs the movements of the machine through a series of electro-mechanical devices. However, the machinery is CNC rather than NC, meaning that the control cabinet on the machine tool itself has an 'editing' facility for 'proving' tapes. Thus faults in programmes can be rectified on the shopfloor during the production of the first component on each new batch. This is done by stopping the machine and rectifying faults in the programme as and when they appear – the control panel having the appropriate devices for this task. (With NC the programme would make frequent trips to and from the office for faults to be rectified.) Corrections are stored in the memory of the machine's own computer, and once 'proved' the rest of the batch is made automatically from the instructions now in the computer memory rather than those on the paper tape. If corrections made have been significant, and if the programme is to be stored for future use – which is frequently the case – then a tape punch can simply be attached to the control cabinet, punching out the modified programme on a fresh paper tape. Thus, next time the same component is required, assuming no design changes in the component, the editing stage is omitted. Five of these machines are turning machines, and the other three are machining centres – used mainly for milling, but also boring, tapping and other functions.

The ninth CNC machine is also a turning machine, but unlike all the others it utilises a prototype manual data input (MDI) control system. In this case the machine has been designed with the intention that programming (as well as proving of programmes as with conventional CNC) may if necessary be carried out at the machine itself, during the production of the first of a batch. This is achieved via the use of a microcomputer in the machine's control cabinet. At the moment, each time a new component is made the computer's memory is wiped clean and the previous programme is lost, but it is intended in the near future to add a device which records the programme for future use on a magnetic cassette tape. With this machine, office programming is eliminated, and proving is effectively carried out during the actual programming.

From this description one might presume it possible to predict the sorts of tasks employees should carry out, and the way the tasks would be divided amongst various functional groups. However, this is a purely technical description of the innovations, and the way CNC is actually applied depends upon certain non-technical considerations.

The Interested Parties

From the beginning, senior management[4] at the plant offered no firm guidelines on the ways in which tasks were to be allocated, and it seems that the present senior management team – and for our purposes the central actors are the managing director, the manufacturing director, and more recently the personnel manager – have inherited a set of working practices which they themselves would not have chosen. (None of these three has been with the firm for more than a few years.) Exactly why previous senior managers had failed to dictate events on the shopfloor remains uncertain, although several long-serving staff did express to me their private views that influence over internal events was, and still is, largely in the hands of the middle management team – their ideas often being at odds with those of the directors. Thus to understand the management input to *current* practices we have to look further down the organisational hierarchy to the middle managers and foremen.

Today some conflict expressed in the form of complaints about 'directors who don't know the machine tool industry' (the recent recruits are in fact ex-motor vehicles industry) or about 'supervisors who can't adapt to change', is occasionally voiced, and indeed one might expect this sort of rift when we note that virtually all the middle managers are long-serving employees, often having risen from the shopfloor and mostly at the peak of their careers (many reaching retirement age within the next ten years or so), while the present directors are the latest of several senior management teams. Without wishing to make a finer point than the evidence allows, one might summarise by saying that the company has two breeds of manager – one careerist and mobile, the other long-serving and loyal – their differing views about work and life-style being expressed in the way they conduct their affairs. This includes, of course, their attitudes and actions towards new technology, and will prove to be relevant as the drama unfolds. The views of middle management, it should be emphasised, are difficult to see as reflections of 'objective' interests, and a strong component of their views appeared to consist of a moral commitment to traditional values of skill and craftsmanship.

The main union is the AUEW, and a closed shop operates. The shop steward system is well organised, and although it may be inappropriate to refer to it as 'strong' given the current market position of the firm, it is recognised at all levels in the firm and carries considerable influence. In the absence of any firm management guidelines, the union could easily ensure that operators on the new machinery were drawn from existing ranks (some machinists were keen to work with the new technology) and that only skilled labour was used. Union concern that only skilled machinists should operate the machinery is not, however, primarily a concern with the tasks people carry out. Rather, it is first and foremost an attempt to ensure that conventional job gradings are continued. As we have already explained, in this plant skill refers to pay and status, as well as to the nature and complexity of tasks, and although the two meanings are not unconnected (it is easier to justify skilled status when the work really is skilled) it is the former which most concerns union officials.[5] The important point here is that skilled labour (in both senses) *is* used, and this has important consequences for the way CNC is utilised.[6] As with other skilled operators in the plant, the CNC operators have, on conventional machines, been accustomed to carrying out both setting and operating.

There are now five programmers, two of them trainees. The last three recruits were internally trained. Most are young with at least some career ambitions. Technical apprenticeships are being undertaken by the two trainees, which are intended to ensure that the programmer gains some experience of machining on the shopfloor as well as programming. They are not, however, recruited from the same source as the machine operators. They have a different status in the company, being represented by a different union (TASS), wearing white coats rather than blue overalls, and so on. (Ironically the most important status difference – that of pay – favours the machine operator rather than the programmer.) Because of the nature of the work, a close relationship with shopfloor operators is inevitable, but these status differences – many of them obvious even to the casual observer – serve to emphasise that a close relationship is not necessarily a congenial relationship.

The final group of actors with a stake in the outcome of the introduction of the new technology were the planners. (In fact, of course, some other groups were involved, but in much more indirect ways.) The planners are the office staff who provide the documentation necessary for manufacture. A major aspect of their work is the provision of planning sheets, which contain information on methods of manufacture (in the case of machining, the type and order of cuts, and so on). As one might guess, shopfloor machinists often refer to them as incompetent 'office wallahs' whose lack of shopfloor experience renders their planning instructions highly suspect and subject to correction, increasing the workload of the machinist, and representing one aspect of the way in which 'management rely on us to get the work out'. Today the planner's work overlaps with that of the programmers too, and one might suspect a similar – if less overt – schism between those two groups, the programmers complaining that their lack of programming experience means their planning sheets are not always appropriate to the needs of CNC machining. There are about six planners, and in the office they contrast sharply with the programmers by their much older age and more sedate behaviour. In fact as a group, the programmers are probably the youngest employees in the firm, as well as being the newest, and in the Manufacturing Facilities Office their age contrasts with all the other groups of staff too.[7]

This outline of the character of the various interested parties should serve to set the scene for the discussion of the evolution of real working practices.

Negotiation of Working Practices

We have already mentioned that the work of the process planner is often questioned by the operator on the shopfloor. With the transfer to computer control the planner's work now goes first to the programmer, whose programme should be written according to the way the planner has decided the job should be done. The planner also decides which jobs are suitable for production on CNC machines – taking into account the size and shape of the component, batch size, and so on. On both these counts, programmers are increasingly attempting to usurp the role of the planner, claiming that they are in a better position to understand the capabilities of modern CNC equipment. A few years ago, according to the programmers, the process planners would not allow programmers any say in planning, but this is now changing, and '. . . we often decide something is not possible and get it changed to our requirements'. Programmers are also encroaching upon the traditional role of the jig and tool draughtsman. When special tools are needed '. . . we design and draw tools ourselves rather than getting the jig and tool draughtsman to draw them'. Thus the present boundaries between these various office functions are the subject of continual re-negotiation with each new piece of work. The indications are that as the programmers establish themselves within the Manufacturing Facilities Office, they are gaining more and more control over wider aspects of preparation for manufacture – a sort of natural job enlargement.

There is a similar negotiation and re-negotiation of tasks between programmers and CNC operators on the shopfloor, and it is this aspect of the change to CNC on which we will concentrate. But dealing with official management policy first – or rather the lack of it – there are no laid down rules for programmers and operators to follow. On introduction of the machinery, management did give the usual assurances about no redundancies through use of the new technology,[8] but neglected to give directions on task allocations. The division of labour has been discussed in meetings between management and worker representatives, but no clear-cut divisions have been settled. (The present senior management team do have plans for the near future, and these will be discussed below, but they play no part in current practices.)

The operators of the CNC machines, as mentioned above, are all skilled machinists. They have, however, each spent only one week in formal training for operating CNC machines. The programmers, on the other hand, have served or are serving lengthy technical apprenticeships geared to the needs of computer control. It thus came as a surprise to learn that operators were getting themselves involved in more than just setting and minding the machines, and eight out of the nine operators were questioned in detail to find out exactly what they were doing. Of these eight, three were in fact carrying out at least some of their own programming, and another four were becoming involved in tape editing (i.e., modifying the programmes which come from the office).

When programmes have been produced in the office, they have to be brought onto the shopfloor and 'proved' at the machine tool itself, and here there is some disagreement over whose tasks it is to do this editing. Also, even after the tape is proved with the first of a batch being satisfactory, operators may still wish to make minor adjustments to the programme – for instance to take account of variations in material quality. The programmers would also wish to question the operators' right to do this. They insist that editing is their own domain, and a battle for control over this important function is carried on. The conflict is symbolised by a key on the control cabinet of each CNC machine, which locks and unlocks the tape editing facility. The programmers would like to take this key away after having proved their own programmes, and to keep full control over use of the machine's control panel. So far, however, operators have managed to keep keys on the shopfloor. Keys never leave the control cabinets, and the real division of tasks, according to one CNC operator, depends on '. . . the circumstances of the job in question, the availability of programmers, and also on personal preferences'. In other words there is an ad hoc re-negotiation of task divisions with each new job, but operators tend to have the upper hand in these negotiations, and in most instances choose for themselves. After four years' operator involvement in editing, this practice is well established, and one could imagine the difficulties in any attempt to change the situation along the lines the programmers advocate.

In a nearby firm which utilises exactly the same CNC turning machines as are used here, tasks are divided not only between programmer and operator, but also between setter and operator, and keys are taken from the control cabinets after proving has been carried out. Here the setter's work is very simple – tooling is pre-set – and the operator's work is even more de-skilled, consisting only of loading/unloading, pressing the on–off switch, and some routine inspection. Information on these practices came to me first from one of the operators in our case study firm, who expressed disapproval of them. Interestingly, it was also mentioned by a programmer as an example of how CNC *should* be used. One engineer from another firm which used this same practice of taking away the key from the control cabinet explained how operators in his experience would go to the trouble of picking the locks to get at the controls. His conclusion was: 'As long as the controls are on the shopfloor, there's no way you will keep operators off them'. (This engineer is now working on a machine tool project at UMIST which will be described below.)

Returning to our case study firm, of the three operators who do some programming, one works on a manual data input lathe which is *designed* for operator programming, and we will refer to this later. The other two work on machining centres, which are designed for *office* programming. One of these operators has worked on his CNC machining centre for four years, and has more or less taught himself how to programme. Starting from an engineering drawing, he programmes the machine using the tape editing facility. This is not the ideal way to programme, and requires some ingenuity, although the operators made it clear that this was not a totally exceptional case, and that they knew of machinists in other plants who had picked up the same skills. This operator had helped teach a younger, recently apprenticed, operator this skill (even today's machinists are not formally taught programming) and the two of them now do the programming for over half the components they make.[9] Management have tacitly recognised the abilities of these operators, and occasionally express their admiration of the work done. The programmers also seem to have accepted an operator input to programming in these cases, and speak of the much-needed lightening of their own workload. In these cases of operator programming on conventional CNC equipment, we are not talking about a simple restructuring or 'reallocation' of the tasks which are given by the hardware. Rather, operators are carrying out tasks which were never intended by the machine designers. Programming at the editing facility is a job which has been *created* by the operators, rather than simply being 'taken on' by them.

Although task divisions are left mainly to the programmers and operators to sort out among themselves, it is no doubt helpful to have some moral support from other groups. The foremen and superintendents on the shopfloor are particularly important here, and probably because they were themselves machinists in the past, they fully sympathise with the arguments of the operators. Their justification for taking up a position supportive of the operators is expressed in terms of technical necessities – for instance programmers do not always produce the tapes quickly enough to keep the machines busy – but also in terms of a '. . . waste of operators' skills if they just stand and watch'. Middle management and foremen thus appeared to express a romantic attachment to what *could* be considered 'out-dated' values of craftsmanship which merely present obstacles to the 'logical' application of technology, and certainly they view the threat to the existence of the skilled machinist with some misgivings. However, their wish that the skills of machinists should not be degraded cannot automatically be written off as uneconomic, and when we come to discuss the arguments surrounding the choice of machine control systems we shall see that there is a healthy economic argument *in favour* of keeping and extending skills.

It may be an exaggeration to call the shopfloor a hostile environment for programmers, and the conflict I observed came only in the form of snubs and cynical comments; but there can be no doubt that the physical location of the editing facilities on the shopfloor gave the machinists a decided advantage in the dispute over who was to carry out editing (and sometimes programming) at the machine. Most people on the shopfloor were supportive of machinists (shop stewards, foremen, superintendents, other machinists), and the shopfloor in this firm was generally still very much the domain of the blue collar worker.

Rationales

In their battle for control, machinists and programmers used economic and technical arguments to justify their own stances. No doubt not all the arguments used were uncovered, but some of the basic ones are summarised overleaf.

All this 'technical knowledge' no doubt carries some logic in its own right. However, the logical argument one chooses is dependent on an underlying political position. The desire for control obviously rests on more than a neutral consideration of technical efficacy, and occasionally the underlying motives would be indicated. For example, the programmers' section leader claimed that:

> . . . CNC gives management more control as to what goes on on the machine . . . once programming is done there should be no way anyone could mess around with it. . . . CNC was designed in the first place because semi-skilled labour is cheaper. . . . Management should decide exactly what the operators' tasks are, and give us full authority for the programmes.

Programmers identify themselves as the new group which should be

Programmers	*Operators*
1 The machines have been designed for separate programming and operating.	1 Machine design allows for operator input.
2 Programmers are trained to prove tapes, and have a better technical ability.	2 Skilled machinists have the best knowledge of actual machining, and thus should be involved in methods by editing tapes.
3 Machinists might be competent on conventional machines but different methods are necessary for CNC. Machinists tend to use out-of-date methods.	3 There is no substitute for shopfloor experience, and new methods can easily be learned.
4 Having written the programme, we have the best knowledge of the component being machined.	4 We have to operate the machines; we need to know the workpiece too. Besides, for many jobs, programming at the machine is possible.
5 Programmers need to see the result of their efforts in the form of finished work in order to learn their job better.	5 If programmers did all this then operators would spend a great deal of time idly standing by. Besides, operator editing means that programmers have more time to spend on their proper task – producing tapes in the office.
6 After proving, the key should be removed to prevent tampering because machining methods have been expertly established.	6 The key must be left at all times so that adjustments can be made to take account of variations in material quality, issue of oversized material, etc.

taking control of manufacturing processes, and obviously feel frustrated – perhaps even threatened – when operators take on what programmers see as their legitimate role. Having recognised the control implications associated with their dominance, one might expect management to support programmers in their struggle to take control out of the hands of shopfloor operators. However, at middle management level the support has gone the other way. Senior managers are somewhat more sympathetic to the programmers' case, as we shall see below, but if any directives have been given on the issue, they have so far failed to filter through to where it counts.

Looking for obvious 'rational' motives, one might expect to discover simple instrumental reasons for the operators' desire to control the work process (especially after considering workers' motives in the rubber moulding company). In fact in relation to CNC machines, Harley Shaiken has cited a case in point.[10] We examine pay later, but note here that operator control of programming or editing in *this* firm offered *no advantages whatsoever* in terms of increasing bonus pay. Rather it seems that a highly skilled and intelligent workforce simply did not wish to hand over the control to which they are accustomed, and accordingly their personal preferences were expressed in terms of 'maintenance of self respect', 'using skills', and 'gaining work satisfaction'. According to one operator, CNC machines '. . . cut your arms off, make you blind, make you deaf, and cut off your sense of feel. . . . These machines de-skilled us – being involved in programming brings some interest back'. And in the words of another, '. . . we still use our skill, and still have our self respect. . . . If they separated programming and operating I would seriously consider finding another occupation'. Indeed, it was the operator who was *least* interested in extending his work beyond machine minding who was most instrumental:

> They're paid to programme, we're paid to operate, and the two should be kept separate until they want to pay me more for the job. . . . No tape, no job. . . . Management will let you start doing programming, but they won't pay you for it.

A few more people within the firm – inside and outside the machine shop – expressed the idea that management were 'taking advantage' of operators who were willing to learn programming without charging the firm for the service. But this is not clearly the case, for although managers *were* obviously on occasions glad of the service, it is equally obvious that *programmers earn less than skilled machinists*. Besides, there was never any *explicit* encouragement even from middle managers.

Operators' measures to maintain control could hardly be referred to as a coordinated 'strategy'. In fact some operators asked *me* how other machinists operated their machines. The machine shop is laid out functionally, meaning that turning machines and machining centres were on different sides of the machine shop, and contact between CNC operators from the turning and milling sections were particularly limited. One presumes that only in the case of an attack on current working practices would the two come together to hammer out a coordinated strategy. However, the stewards *had* been known to prevent programmers from making changes to machine controls when requested to by individual operators, and this was sufficient to keep operators happy and for programmers to complain that '. . . there is too much resistance on the shopfloor'.

Technical Constraints

So far we have not discussed any constraints on working practices imposed by the hardware employed. But these obviously do exist, and do place some limits on the amount of control an operator can exert. This point is best displayed by contrasting the three types of CNC machine used – i.e., the manual data input lathe, the machining centres, and the turning machines. Taking the MDI lathe first, the operator does all the programming, setting and operating. The operator in this case was given two weeks of intensive instruction by the machine supplier, and has since then managed the machine on his own initiative. On the machining centres, operators are always involved in tape proving, but do only about two thirds of the programming. On the turning machines operators rarely do programming, and sometimes programmers prove their own tapes. The differences between the three are to do with design of the machine tools – i.e., some facilitate shopfloor programming far better than others – though of course the firm is not simply at the mercy of any particular designers: the firm can choose between different machines and machine control systems. Before looking at the processes involved in choosing between CNC systems, however, and to emphasise the fact that this section on use of technology is not dealing only with peripheral or unimportant work practices which are 'largely determined', let us make a contrast. First recall the operator on the machining centre who carries out all his own tape proving, and the majority of his own programming, then compare this practice with the following quote from the capital justification for the *very same machining centre*, written by a production engineer, and representing the expectations placed on the hardware:

> The further use of CNC in the machine shop will reduce the need for operator skill. With the present shortage of skilled operators, this is particularly important. Further, by taking the control of the machining away from the operator a more consistent performance will result.

Shopfloor Inputs to Technical Design

The quote from the capital justification above should now be contrasted with the following comment from another capital justification for a very similar CNC machining centre, but written by a different production engineer. Here, among the list of advantages of its control system is: 'Far easier to programme on the shopfloor'. (This particular machine is yet to be sanctioned by the directors, but the production engineer who wrote the justification suggested it may soon be given the go-ahead.) This justification of basically similar machines on opposite grounds reflects the flexibility of some modern CNC equipment, the choice of hardware not determining tasks. In fact if we include *human tasks* in our definition of technology, we must recognise the relevant actors in the firm as playing an important part in actually *designing* that technology. This is not simply to say that tasks can be combined in different ways, which is really job enlargement, but that *the tasks themselves* are still to be determined, even given all the hardware. If operators do some tape proving, or if programmers design and draw their own tools, all that happens is a transfer of tasks from one occupational group to another – the tasks themselves remain the same. However, when operators programme at the machine itself, the tasks themselves change, and we are talking about *a redefinition of technology*. Programming at the machine means using equipment ostensibly intended only for editing, and bypassing the programming facilities in the office. Operator programming, then, is a profoundly different 'way of doing' something, representing *a profoundly different technology*. Thus when the two production engineers are considering the same machining centre, they may in an important way be conceptualising different technologies. (Another example of technology being re-defined by real working practices occurs when operators use the manual override on the older NC machines. This facility is intended only for exceptional use, and its everyday use effectively means that NC machining technology has become conventional machining technology.)

The contrast between programmer-programming and operator-programming is also the contrast between what we have called conventional CNC and manual data input (MDI) CNC. By striving to become involved in programming through taking advantage of editing facilities, operators have implicitly been creating an MDI technology, and although existing hardware places limits on the development of this practice, the achievements of operators could hardly be trivialised. Here is a case where workers themselves, with the support of *some* managers, are involved in redirecting the technology in ways which recognise, use and develop human skills. They have begun to *create a tradition* of technology and work which is a viable alternative to the de-skilling and de-grading technology which some would attempt to impose. But there are limits, especially on the turning machines, and thus we must look at the choice of technology as a constraint on working practices.

Choice of Machine Tools

Not only production engineers are involved in choosing equipment. What happens is that in policy meetings involving the manufacturing director and various others – the head of Manufacturing Facilities, the machining superintendent, a production engineer, and sometimes the managing director (participation depends on the size and nature of the capital expenditure) – it is decided that a new machine is needed to do a particular job. Brochures and other information are collected, and the various engineers and managers decide between them the machine they think will be most suitable. A capital justification is drawn up by a production engineer, and this then goes for sanction to the directors. One production engineer stated that:

> With justifications, we look at machines against the type of work anticipated, then justify them solely on the grounds of costs – payback periods and so on. . . . It's very important to get the right man for the job, otherwise production suffers. But we get the machine first, *then* the operator. . . . If we don't have the right one we'll go outside to find him.

This implies that the firm buys the machinery, then deals with the social consequences later, and such justifications make very dry reading, referring rarely to the character of employees. However, the quotes from the justifications stated above do show some concern with the type of work machines might create. Certainly, before the capital justifications are written there is a good deal of informal discussion and deliberation, giving grounds for suspicion that formal justifications could be 'post hoc' technical rationalisations which tend to play down the social and political considerations which go into them. If and when more MDI machines become available, then we may expect a strong push by middle management towards this technology, but not necessarily to see it reflected in formal documents as a social choice.

Certainly management and engineers at all levels are beginning to recognise that there is a choice to be made. A production engineer sums it up: 'The firm has to go one of two ways. We can either retain skill on the shopfloor and have manual data input, or transfer skill into here with more tape control machines.'

Machine Tool Design

But given all this, *availability* of MDI is still a problem which is bound to place limits on management choices, and it is thus important for us to examine machine tool design at the supplying firm in order to fully understand the way technology and skills might develop within this firm. An empirical examination of machine tool design along the lines of this research would probably prove highly fruitful – for if it is necessary to understand the social context of application to understand technology, it is doubtless also necessary to understand the social context of research and development. This is outside the scope of this research project, but fortunately we can refer to some work currently being carried out at the Machine Tool Division's laboratories at the University of Manchester Institute of Science and Technology, which is directly relevant.[11]

Here an MDI lathe had already been successfully developed which is similar to the prototype lathe in our case study firm. The nature of jobs with this system have been considered during its design, and the result is an 'interactive' microcomputer control which allows the operator to programme the machine during the production of the first of a batch. It is assumed that a conventionally-skilled machinist will be the operator, as is often the case in small and medium batch production.[12] Professor Rosenbrock and others, from the Institute and elsewhere, are now engaged in a research programme in which a complete flexible manufacturing system (including a robot, an NC milling machine and an NC lathe) will be designed to allow for operator programming on the shopfloor. It will take advantage of the machinist's existing metal cutting skills, and extend his skills to include computer programming. At the same time as being developed with commercial applications in mind, the opportunity is to be taken to study the ways in which work designs are 'built in' to the technology, and how these can be influenced by social scientists or other interested parties at the development stage of the technology.

The results of this research should give valuable insights into the development of MDI, and hopefully also to the social forces behind the general direction which CNC technology is taking and will take in the future. At present machine shops such as our case study firms are in the position where their future technological development is uncertain. Much depends on the direction of machine tool design, which is at least partly in the hands of others.[13]

Future Directions of the Firm

Senior management have so far had little direct influence on the development of new working customs and practices.[14] Yet since their arrival they have been formulating ideas on where the company should go with regard to machining technology. Basically, the manufacturing director would like to create a new grade of 'section leaders' (or 'leading hands') who would be responsible for groups of CNC machines. Rather than being a chargehand, the section leader would be a 'supergrade' of machinist – his skills and responsibilities being recognised by a new pay grade. Being the technical expert for a group of machines, he would be responsible for tape proving, and assuring machines were correctly set, production runs smoothly, and so on. This would '. . . release the programmer from the shopfloor so that he could concentrate on producing tapes' (tape shortages are currently a major problem) at the same time as '. . . de-skilling the work of the operator', who would now be basically a machine minder. The source of section leaders would be from among those skilled machinists who have taught themselves some programming and are obviously competent at the control panel: 'When you get a worker who tells the *programmer* how to do his job, you want to make better use of his abilities'. With the shiftworking which is envisaged, and with the expansion of CNC equipment which should come shortly, it should be possible to use all or most of the present CNC operators as section leaders.

The machining superintendent pointed out that the section leader ideas already operate to some extent informally. In particular, both training and advice are given to newer CNC operators by the more experienced ones. However, initial moves to formalise and extend the idea have so far been met with resistance by the union, which is 'against the creation of an elite', and implementation would be particularly difficult in the current context of short-time working and redundancies. The reorganisation ideas have thus for the time being been shelved.

One million pounds is to be made available for new machinery by the American owners this year – specifically for equipment necessary to produce one of their domestic products for the European market. Much of this new machinery is to be CNC, and will presumably provide better opportunities for reorganisation. What is likely to happen is difficult to say. The positions of the various groups have been outlined, and we can expect some disagreements, but so far differences have not been expressed in overt ways. It is tempting to predict, and it is tempting to urge particular directions to be taken, but neither will be attempted here. Suffice it to have shown that there are choices to be made, and the mechanisms through which those choices operate.

Shifts and Payment

Two major aspects of work organisation shown to be important in some of the case studies – shifts and payment – have not been discussed. Shifts have not been discussed because none are worked. But it is worth mentioning here that many of the CNC machines were justified on the basis of shiftworking, and that their payback periods are greatly increased because of this under-utilisation. This point is, of course, significant in management's desire to introduce shiftwork again in the future, and as such represents one way in which the technology may affect the working patterns of shopfloor workers.

The payment system has not been discussed because at present it does not influence, and is not influenced by, the CNC technology. A bonus system does operate, and one could expect this to affect the way operators work the machines. Certainly, on hearing of operators insisting on keeping keys to control panels, I half-expected to see operators using this as an opportunity to adjust speeds and feeds to higher rates than the time-study man believed were being used. One of the methods engineers in fact related one instance of this from the past. This is not the case today. Because of the current shortage of work for CNC, and also because of the lack of planned times for jobs on CNC, the tendency is for operators to be given a 'planned' time (for the purposes of bonus calculations) for the *actual* time it takes to do the job, regardless of the work done, assuring maximim bonus is recorded. The payment system does, however, become important in our discussion of the new shop scheduling system, and a full explanation of its mechanics will be found in the next chapter.

8 The Machine Tool Manufacturer – Shop Scheduling

Chapter seven has described the social and political aspects of the new production machinery being introduced in this firm. This chapter examines the attempted computerisation of the system of progress chasing.

As we shall see, the new system of organising and controlling the flow of work around the shopfloor had implications wider than the effect on the work of the progress clerks, and in particular cannot be properly understood apart from the payment system and the whole system of production control. However, my interest in shop scheduling began with the changing role of the progress clerks, and we will begin this section with a discussion of their work.

The Progress Chaser

The progress clerk, or 'chaser', has until recently played a role in the firm which has hardly changed for decades. Some of the chasers have been with the firm for most of their working lives, are now nearing retirement age, and they have seen no basic changes until the current one. In the summer of 1980 there were nine progress chasers. One retired but was not replaced, so that in October when the new system was introduced there were eight. Their union is the AUEW, and they have a section steward to represent them. They share one office in the centre of the shopfloor, and apart from the fact that they have a desk each, they are barely distinguishable from other shopfloor workers. In this respect they stand apart from the other technical and office workers in the company, whose different status is emphasised by the wearing of white coats, being members of a different trade union (TASS), and so on.[1] The progress chasers' pay grade is one lower than skilled machinists – they are recognised as semi-skilled workers. Of the eight progress clerks one is a woman, who keeps the records in order, and apart from the tea ladies who venture into the shop twice a day, she is the only woman one is likely to see on the shopfloor. There is a supervisor in charge of these eight progress clerks, and he has an office which is adjacent to theirs. The door between the two offices is never closed, and the supervisor is constantly interrupted by the chasers who come with a host of problems, and by the foremen from the various sections of the shop who want to know where this or that piece of work is, and so on.

The division of labour among progress chasers was previously based on end products – meaning that each chaser would be responsible for ensuring that all parts necessary for a particular machine, or group of machines, were on schedule. This would involve checking that the right parts were in stock, or at least on order in the purchasing department, and that 'made-in' items were on schedule for completion by the date they were due to be assembled. Most time was spent chasing made-in items, which generally have to travel around several different sections of the machine shop for various functions to be performed on them – e.g., turning, milling, boring, drilling, tapping, etc. A record of the movements of the various components was kept in the office, to enable an immediate check on the location of the items necessary to build any particular machine. All this meant that the progress chasers had a detailed knowledge of certain machines, and a detailed knowledge of the whole machine shop, both being necessary for them to perform their work properly.

Problems with the Progress System

One of the major problems with this system, and in fact a major impetus to changing the system, was that because work was allocated by machine, the progress clerks would chase their own parts around different sections of the shop without due regard to the needs of other progress chasers. Thus the foremen responsible for the different sections of the shop (milling, turning, etc.) would be under pressure from several different progress chasers demanding that their own parts be made and moved on quickly. There would thus be a tendency for work of low priority to be dealt with before more urgent requirements, and this led to shortages of parts for the machine assemblers. This problem has been recognised by the company for many years. For instance a company document written over ten years ago comments that '. . . of 50 components in a sub-assembly, 5 would not be available when required'. A great deal of time would thus be spent 'fire fighting' – with foremen, individual fitters and superintendents as well as progress clerks chasing urgently required parts. Apart from machines not being built on schedule, there would often be an ad hoc splitting of batches, and a tendency to switch workers more frequently from one job to another – the resulting inefficiencies being considerable.

An attempt to remedy the situation was the introduction of a priority list system. Each section foreman would have a list of work which was top priority. These jobs were derived from shortages at the fitting stage, and were placed on the lists by the progress clerks, who liaised closely with the fitting foremen. However, the effectiveness of this system soon declined. As one foreman explained, '. . . it was alright when it first started but after a bit, and if the shop had got a big workload on . . . in next to no time you've got sheets and sheets, so it doesn't mean a thing' – the progress clerks were beginning to put everything they wanted onto the sheets, regardless of urgency. Thus a 'super-priority' system was attempted – green stamps being placed next to those items which really were urgent. According to the same foreman: 'That went alright for a bit until these lads realised that by putting a green stamp on they got it quick, so they were putting bloody green stamps on the lot!' Two green stamps were tried next, and later two separate lists were used – one for 'really urgent' fitting requirements; the latter system was used until the recent change to shop scheduling, and has worked reasonably well. This was partly because of a better understanding between fitting, progress and machining sections, but also because the recent decline in output meant a smaller number of urgent fitting requirements.

The problem described above is a part of the more general problem of high levels of work in progress, which has obvious financial implications, and is the central motive behind the new scheduling system. It is hoped that the new system will allow the turning over of stock and work in progress twice a year instead of once.

Shop Scheduling

Basically, the new system of shop scheduling is a transfer from a division of labour by group of products to a division of labour by section area on the shopfloor. Now, instead of being responsible for a group of machines, the progress clerks (now known as 'shop schedulers') are responsible for a particular section of the shop (e.g., grinding and gear cutting, the heavy bays, the turning section, etc.). For most sections there is now one foreman and one shop scheduler, and they are supposed to work together in assuring that the right job is done at the right time. The changes are illustrated on page 75. Priorities, instead of being decided by fitting foremen and progress chasers, are now given on computer print-outs. The necessary information, taken from work tickets, is collected by the production control staff and fed into a computer which is programmed to produce all the instructions necessary for jobs to be properly scheduled. The information comes back to the schedulers once a week in the form of computer print-outs, called 'work centre schedules'. The foremen also receive copies. These schedules give a priority rating in terms of figures for each component or workpiece which is to pass through that particular work centre in

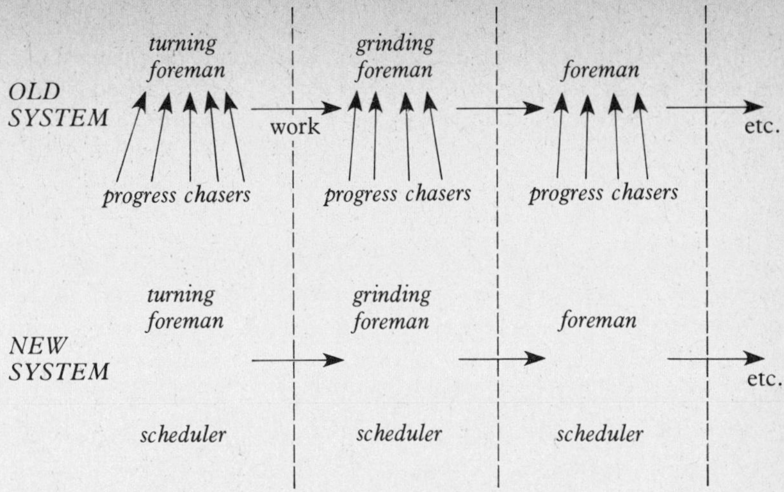

the near future – the lower the figure the higher the priority. The schedulers explained that 'as a rule of thumb' the minus figures are urgent, those below one are important, and those above one can wait. Each piece of work carries with it a 'travel document', containing machining instructions, batch quantity, etc., and these are collected in boxes at each section of the shop as and when work arrives after previous operations. The scheduler can now simply arrange these according to the priority rating given on the work centre schedules, and the foreman can ensure that the urgent work is done first.

As we shall see, the system has not worked out in practice in such a straightforward and simple way, and to some extent old methods are still relied upon, but the schedulers have now experienced the new system sufficiently to form some opinions on it. Before looking at the problems of the new scheduling system, and before examining its wider ramifications (assuming that its problems are not insurmountable), we shall see what these opinions are.

From Progress Chaser to Shop Scheduler

The schedulers are unanimous in their opinions on the new computerised system. The old system is preferred to the new. Instead of taking responsibility for a whole machine or group of machines, and chasing every part necessary for its production, the scheduler simply receives a list of priorities for a particular section of the machine shop, and sees that the coded instructions from the computer are fulfilled.

With the old system, '. . . you become a part of that machine . . . you're doing something constructive. When you see a machine being built you're achieving something', and '. . . I could walk up a section and see from a distance what I'm looking for. I knew exactly what the parts I needed looked like and where I'd be likely to find them'. With the new system, however, '. . . everything becomes a number on a priority basis. The new system only tells us numbers and priorities . . . now it's just numbers, it don't mean a thing'.

The expression of production needs in terms of codes and numbers is totally new to the progress chasers, and they accept the new way of doing things only with reluctance. An often amusing, but telling, aspect of their treatment of the new system is the constant attempt to translate figures and codes into tangible events and physical objects. For instance, when one day I was following a scheduler as he went about his daily business[2] we somehow found our way into the production control department. 'What's P2?' he asked one of the data processing personnel. 'The P's are the buyers' came the reply. 'So who's P2?' he shouted out loud. There was no reply this time, but we now went up to the buying department where he asked again: 'Who's P2?' The buyers looked a little embarrassed, but one owned up to being P2. 'And what number are you, Sheila?' asked the scheduler as he turned to another buyer.

Other examples are the translation of code numbers into particular production machines on the shopfloor, or into components, subassemblies, etc. But of course it is impossible to turn *all* these *abstract* figures into *tangible* persons or things, and in the end the scheduler has to learn to deal with numbers which 'don't mean a thing'.

Schedulers also talked about the loss of responsibility with the new system. Previously, when target dates were not met and shortages appeared during assembly, '. . . the fitting foreman would have someone to attack – we knew whose fault it was'. But now there are likely to be several schedulers involved in the production of any particular component (the component may have to be milled, drilled, tapped, ground, etc.) so that 'no one person is answerable'.

The work is also obviously far simpler and far more tedious – the computer programme now doing the locating of work in progress as well as determining priorities and monitoring movements; and also more impersonal – 'crunching numbers' is not the same as working and negotiating with the foremen.[3]

All in all the transition from progress chaser to shop scheduler has been an unpleasant one, but then '. . . that's modernisation, isn't it?'

Problems with the Scheduling System

After seven months the scheduling system still did not work, and one had to wonder whether the 'teething problems' were not really deep faults. The schedulers still relied on the old system to a large extent – exactly how we shall see later – and certainly they believed (or at least hoped) that the new system could never work: their numbers and priorities '. . . nine times out of ten are wrong', and one explanation was that: '. . . there are too many small batch parts for too many machines for this system to work. It might be OK in a car plant'. In fact there are likely to be a host of reasons why the information coming from production control was inaccurate, but one of the main reasons was the poor quality of information going in. Here perhaps the major factor – and certainly the one factor which management were aware of and the schedulers acting upon – was the way the payment system was being worked by machinists and assemblers on the shopfloor. Indeed it is difficult to understand the scheduling system at all apart from the payment system, and an explanation of its workings may be useful.

Until 1973 the firm operated a piecework system, requiring twelve ratefixers to establish and negotiate times.[4] Between 1973 and 1976 there was a simple hourly rate, with no bonuses at all. From the end of 1976 a group bonus scheme was devised; this still operates today and is based on the work done by operators and fitters, but most other employees do benefit by receiving percentages of the bonus earned – for instance shop schedulers receive 50% of the bonus achieved. Given the 'group' basis of bonus pay, it may seem a little strange that bonus calculations are only indirectly related to overall output – individual operators still being measured as under the old piecework system – but this is the case, and exactly how it operates is as follows:

A 'performance' is calculated each month by dividing total issued time by total clocked time (these 'total' times are those for direct labour only – i.e., operators and fitters):

$$\text{Performance} = \frac{\text{Issued time}}{\text{Clocked time}} \times 100\%$$

The bonus payment threshold is 63%, and for every percentage point above that a bonus of £1 per week is paid – up to a maximum of £15. 'Issued time' is the time which comes from the planner's office with the work ticket, and 'clocked time' is time worked (taken from clocking-in cards). Thus the nearer workers get to issued times, the higher the performance.

Many of the issued times have been established by time and motion studies, or by agreements between ratefixers and operators. But for the last seven years or so no proper 'ratefixing' has been done, and thus some of the issued times are just planners' estimates. In these cases any extra time taken to do the job is automatically given a 'variance code', and the total time recorded counts as the issued time (i.e., the planned time) *regardless of the real time taken*. (Variance codes represent excuses for spending more time than estimated for particular jobs – e.g., faulty castings, incorrect drawings, machine breakdown, etc. – and there are over a hundred of these.) However, most of the variance codes are excluded from bonus calculations. The clocked time used for calculations is also reduced accordingly so that there is no effect on the calculation. Operators, of course, often try to convince ratefixers that the extra time they took falls into one of the bonus paying variance categories, and no longer being involved in establishing times on the shopfloor, the ratefixers are at a disadvantage in negotiating variance codes and times. Operators are thus tending to get what they want written into these variances more frequently than one would normally expect. Management have recognised this as a problem, and intend to give the foremen the responsibility of adding variance codes and times to work tickets, since foremen 'know what is really going on'.[5]

Also the code numbers used are to be reduced in number to six, in line with the coding system in operation in the US firms. Thus when information from the work tickets is compiled and sorted by a central computer, the US parent company will be able to see at a glance exactly where inefficiencies lie. For instance, if the variance code representing machine breakdown is frequently used, this may suggest the need for more preventive maintenance, etc.

At the same time as individual operators and fitters seek to increase the recorded 'issued time' going into the bonus calculation, the stewards somehow manage to gather and record information on the development of bonus pay for the month. When the ceiling of £15 is reached some work tickets are 'banked', to be submitted for the following month. In this way workers can control their bonus pay from month to month,[6] and have in fact managed to achieve the full £15 for several months running now. In fact they hope that management may now raise the bonus ceiling to allow them to earn more.

It is precisely this 'kitty' of work tickets which leads to inaccurate information being fed into the computer in production control – for information from the same tickets is being used by production control to tell the computer when a particular piece of work is complete, and when it has moved onto the next operation. Thus the work centre schedules coming back from production control are bound to be inaccurate and out of date, and the schedulers have to rely on the old system to 'botch up' the new.

Botching up the System

With the old progress system, the woman who dealt with records always used inspection tickets (which are blue) rather than work tickets (which are white) to update information in the progress books. She has continued to do this throughout the implementation of the new system. The blue tickets are signed by inspectors immediately on satisfactory completion of any particular operation, and are left in boxes at work stations. Every morning these are collected by the progress clerk, and entered into the progress books, so that the exact position of work in progress can be seen for each machine. Each week when the work centre schedules arrive from production control they are 'updated' from the information gathered by the old manual recording method. Each scheduler has to spend at least several hours every Thursday carrying out this laborious task.

Schedulers also maintain the old system to some extent through habit – they still tend to '. . . keep an eye out for our old machines', and when parts go missing the easiest and quickest way of finding them is still through the scheduler's tacit knowledge. However, these skills now being officially redundant, the schedulers complain that they are gradually losing their old habits, and wonder what will happen if the system fails to work before their old abilities are forgotten altogether.

An explicit recognition that the scheduling system was failing was indicated by management in December 1980 when two of the schedulers were allocated the full-time task of dealing with fitting shortages. Liaising with the fitting foremen, they compile 'critical shortages' lists, and pass them to the appropriate schedulers who ensure they are given priority treatment at the work stations – a familiar practice!

One wonders why production control do not use the blue tickets in favour of the white tickets as their information input, but the only explanation gained was that '. . . the blue tickets are going to be phased out in the near future, so we might as well get used to the white ones'. Using white tickets certainly means standardising practice in line with the US system, but one cannot help seeking a more convincing explanation than bureaucratic tidiness.[7]

Despite all this, scheduling is going ahead, and one must ask what will happen to the scheduler himself, presuming that the system is made to work – in particular by making the bonus system work once again. The schedulers already recognise the system's potential for making them 'replaceable': '. . . anybody can do the new job'. But also, as one scheduler put it: '. . . they might want to put us on the dole queue – eliminate progress men altogether'. Schedulers have been told that they will take on the new tasks of allocating work to machine operators, recording it when completed, and handing out more work, etc. However, the schedulers feel that the foreman is the person with the best knowledge of the capabilities of operators, and thus best able to decide who should get which job. Thus they see this as possibly being a temporary measure, to be phased out as and when foremen are persuaded to become their own schedulers.

But whether or not the scheduler (or anyone else) is employed for this task, we can now see the bringing together of the progress function and the payment system at the point of production, the monitoring and control of both now being in the hands of a foreman with greatly enlarged responsibilities. Exactly how these new responsibilities will be dealt with is to be seen.

Management Control

Taken together, the changes in the payment system and in progress reporting represent an attempt by management to gain control over what goes on on the shopfloor. In particular, by making foremen responsible for completing variance codings on work tickets, and by eliminating the progress chaser as such, management control over production becomes more direct through the management hierarchy, rather than through a progress system and through industrial engineering. It is only in this context that the new computerised shop scheduling system can be understood. It is not simply a new technology which has come along and affected the workplace. It was actually introduced and used for control purposes – it is in fact a control technology. Of course, it is not easy to refer to this need for control either in a straightforward political sense, nor as a simple technical necessity – it is of course both: the economic and technical need for better control was obvious (high levels of work in progress, etc.), but the actual form the new system takes is dependent on a host of political factors.

Senior managers at the plant have been responsible for installing the new control systems, and if and when the systems work, the advantages to them will be great – control over production would be more directly in their hands. However, this control is first dependent on getting the workforce to give up its own control of the bonus payments, with regard to both variance codings and work ticket kitties. This is hardly a straightforward task. Also, it would mean more generally that the performances of middle managers and foremen could be measured 'objectively' by reference to production figures – a situation one might expect middle managers to be reluctant to accept. Thus achievement of control is highly problematic, and the outcome in terms of working systems is by no means given.

The efficient functioning of the systems also means that in turn the US parent company can more easily measure the performance of this UK subsidiary, and can even have a breakdown of figures which points out to them exactly where any 'inefficiencies' lie. In particular, the rationalisation of the variance coding system can probably be seen as part of the US owners' attempts to do their own detailed financial monitoring, especially when placed in the context of a more general imposition of their complete costing system. Thus the direction the control technology takes must now also be seen in the light of the needs of the American owners – and one might expect their impact to become more apparent over the next two or three years.

In the context of what was said about the differences between senior management and middle management at the plant, one can perhaps understand the attempts by senior managers to gain more control. Similarly, in the context of the circumstances in which the Americans took over this company (falling sales, recession in machine tools, etc.), one can understand why the Americans wish to rationalise, and to control that rationalisation. Access was not possible to the sort of 'top level' information which would allow a thorough analysis of the motives of the most senior managers, and thus 'corporate strategies' must remain largely unexplained. We *have* shown, however, that the implementation of new means of *formal* control are highly problematic, being dependent on, and influenced by, the existing *informal* control systems. One must understand these existing systems in order to properly understand motives, and in order to understand eventual outcomes.

9 The Politics of Technical Change

The case studies invariably show that managers, engineers and workers become involved in orienting the 'impact' of new technology in particular directions, and that there are conflicts of interests, occasionally expressed openly, between the various interested parties – between managers and workers, between different groups of workers, and also between different individual managers or groups of managers. Although the resolution of these conflicts occurs largely through information channels, processes of social choice and political negotiation are clearly in evidence, and are shown to have a profound effect on the nature of technical change in each firm. Before discussing the social and political dimensions however, it is worth pointing out how the case studies shed some light on the practical role of the technical and efficiency aspects of new technology, since these are frequently assumed to be the major, if not the sole, considerations in technical change. The case studies show how the significance of 'efficiency' may in fact be other than is normally assumed.

Efficiency: Objective Measure or Ideological Justification?

The first point to be made about 'efficiency', 'product quality', 'productivity', etc., is that these, generally unquestioned, indicators of technological success are difficult to measure with any degree of accuracy, and in any case are rarely measured in sufficient detail to determine the exact economic advantages over any alternatives. Of course, *formal* (written) justifications of capital expenditure may make elaborate comparisons of productivity, capital costs, payback periods, etc., between, for instance, alternative new machines. These justifications were used frequently, according to most accounts, as the basis of decisions on choice of technology in many of the case study firms. But it is probably safe to say that in no instance could it be demonstrated that *in practice* the new technology met the measured expectations of the production engineer who 'justified' the technology, or of the machine supplier who advertised it. Besides, measures of the *actual* economic returns of new processes were invariably in the form of 'two or three times more output per man', or 'it paid for itself in about two years', rather than the pounds and pence, and hours and minutes, of the pre-implementation assessment. In practice then, there was simply no accurate measure of productivity gains or of comparative improvements in efficiency.[1]

The point being made here is not that new technology *in general*, nor even electronic control of batch production in general, can be questioned on the grounds of efficiency *relative to conventional* (non-automated) technology – though in some instances it can.[2] Rather, the important point is that the ambiguous and imprecise nature of the measurement of performance means that choices between alternative available designs and the way they are used (the way work is organised) cannot be explained simply in terms of technical and economic advantages. Where engineers and managers *do* use these explanations one must remain suspicious and expect to find additional motives.

There is always more than 'one best way'. This does not mean that *all* technical designs and working practices are technically and economically feasible. But it does mean that technical and economic considerations serve only to *constrain* the possible options. For instance, in the case of the machine tool manufacturer, the choice between manual data input (MDI) and conventional CNC – two very different designs – was not one between *technical* superiority and inferiority, but between 'retaining skill on the shopfloor' and 'transferring skill into the office'. As the case study makes clear, the *availability* of MDI imposes constraints on choice – if it is not available it cannot be chosen – but on purely technical and economic grounds, as far as is measurable, it is the equal of conventional CNC. Similarly, throughout the case studies, it was shown how the working practices which evolved around new equipment and processes, although not independent of technical and economic constraints, were never completely determined by them. For instance, in the plating company we showed how the working practices which the platers preferred – especially the more frequent use of the manual override – were not those intended by management. But it could not be shown in a straightforward way that the practices advocated by management were in any sense more efficient. To the independent observer, neither the platers' emphasis on quality nor the management's emphasis on quantity appeared illogical with regard to performance considerations. In engineering terms they were, as far as one could see, equal.

The success of *any* engineering project is of course extremely difficult to measure, but when discussing the introduction of new technology into the *workplace* one must bear in mind the central problem of the inclusion of 'labour' in any calculations. For unless one assumes the total acquiescence of workers, one must recognise that performance depends on the acceptance and proper use of new equipment by a workforce which has particular values, interests, objectives, motivations, and so on. Throughout, the case studies show how workers became involved in establishing precise working arrangements, and thus, of course, the performance – the economic returns – of the new technology. Just to give two straightforward instances: in the machine tool manufacturer, workers were currently resisting attempts by management to introduce shiftwork for CNC machines[3] – yet the machines had been justified on the grounds that shiftwork would allow a short pay-back period. And in the plating firm, the productivity of the new automated lines depended not least on the working practices which evolved. *After* implementation managers were highly aware of this fact. Little wonder then, that pre-implementation measures of efficiency are likely to turn out inaccurate – 'labour' does not lend itself to simple measurement (or as Braverman would have it, the translation of 'labour power' into 'labour' is always problematic).

Given these qualifications – that measurement is inaccurate, that there is always more than 'one best way', and that the acquiescence of labour cannot be assured – one must question the real role of 'efficiency' arguments in technical change. In fact, what our case studies show is that arguments about the efficiency of new production technologies can serve as *scientific glosses which conceal or obscure the political considerations* which have gone into decisions on technical change and work organisation. In other words, arguments from efficiency can be *used* by the various interest groups *in order to justify, or make legitimate, choices which are essentially political*, both in motivation and consequence. In the plating company, for example, management's claim that a lower quality and a higher scrap rate could be tolerated, and that improvements in total output were most important, coincided with the fact that the achievement of these ends would entail workers giving up control over the immediate production process, and allowing themselves to be subject to more rigorous pacing by the machinery. Since these latter effects had earlier been mentioned by managers as basic objectives in automation, one must question whether the performance argument played more than an ideological role.

One might expect that managers and engineers, because of their superior education and training, would always be able to win any ideological battles with workers about the efficiency of particular technologies and the working practices associated with them. Certainly at an *official* level it was normally the case that workers accepted management's designs – workers simply did not see the technical aspects of work as matters for their concern. It was left to managers to determine what was 'efficient', and workers became involved only when areas which they *did* see as their legitimate concerns were affected – generally meaning, at the most, redundancy, manning levels, demarcations and payment. Almost invariably in the case study firms, trade unions and workers' committees became involved in technical change only to the extent that the change impinged on *traditional collective bargaining issues*. This raises some very important questions which will be dealt with in chapter ten.

Unofficially, however, workers did become involved in important ways in technical matters – especially when it came to the establishment of working practices – and exactly how will be discussed in detail below. The point to note here is that even though workers *were* at an enormous disadvantage, they did manage on occasions to construct their own arguments about the efficiency of their own preferred methods. The platers mentioned above are a good case in point, but even more impressive were the arguments generated by the programmers and operators in the machine tool manufacturing firm during their battle for control of the function of editing programmes.

Workers generated arguments, however, only at the implementation stage of innovation. The design and choice of technology were thus unquestionably management prerogatives, their technological choices rarely being considered matters for union or worker concern. Even at the implementation stage it was managers who used economic justifications most seriously and most frequently, and it was thus generally the case that their arguments were accepted. In fact in the machine tool manufacturing firm, where workers were winning the 'battle for control' over programmers, and justifying their stance on economic grounds, there were no clear instructions on working practices from top management, and operators were generally supported by middle managers and foremen. If management support was strongly on the side of programmers, one might wonder how well and for how long the operators' arguments could stand up.[4] Generally speaking it was managers who made most use of efficiency arguments in order to justify intentions which were often political in nature, and certainly managers were in the best position to do so – it was, after all, part of their job. Workers' use of efficiency arguments could thus be precarious, since faith in them, in a sense, plays into management hands.

In at least two of the four more detailed case studies – in the plating company and in the rubber moulding company – one of the underlying political motivations of managers was to take control of production away from machine operators. It is not difficult, therefore, to understand why an ideology which makes this process appear to be an inevitable part of a technical change pursued for purely economic reasons appeals to managers. If consensus can be achieved on the notion that a particular choice of technical and social organisation is most efficient, it does not necessarily follow that workers will conform to management demands, but it certainly helps. After all, generally speaking workers and their representatives do show at least some concern that their employing organisations remain competitive.[5] The most alarming instance of the unquestioned acceptance of new technology was the new shop scheduling system which dramatically changed the role of progress clerks in an extremely de-grading manner. Their resigned acceptance of the new methods was summed up in the comment '. . . that's modernisation, isn't it?' In the other cases, economic justifications were generally convincing at an official level. Actual working practices on the shopfloor, however, were another matter.

Of course, management intentions are not *necessarily* to de-skill or wrest control – a point we shall return to in the next chapter. For instance, the optical company management voluntarily instigated a system of job rotation and improved working conditions. Here managers referred to increased worker satisfaction, a happier place to come to in the morning, and so on. But also, as if to make their humanistic concerns legitimate, they referred to the economic advantages of job rotation (shiftwork is possible, holidays are easily covered, etc.). And even the psychological advantages themselves were connected to economic benefits (less mistakes through inattention, decreased absenteeism, etc.). Management's use of the efficiency argument is thus not *always* sinister and consciously underhand. Rather, it seems that in part, managers feel most secure when all their actions can be justified in terms of increased performance.

Important though they are, this is not the place to go into great depth on the general philosophical questions about the nature of efficiency and its relationship to technological change which have inevitably been raised. Rather, we have shown how efficiency can be used as an ideological tool which legitimates social and political choices. We can now concern ourselves with the ways in which the values and interests of the actors involved help guide technical changes in particular directions, and the way these interests become embodied in the technical and social organisation of work.

Stages of Innovation

The sequence of the assessment will be under the categories of the design, choice, and implementation and debugging of new technology. Each of these stages in the process of innovation will be shown to provide junctures at which actors can (and do) intervene to influence the direction of change and its organisational effects. It should, of course, be borne in mind that the distinctions between these stages are for analytical purposes only, and as the case studies made perfectly clear, are not empirically grounded. On the other hand, we must also emphasise that the distinctions between the stages of innovation which *are* made are especially useful in relation to the automation of *batch* production rather than other types of automation. With the automation of process production (chemicals, oil refineries, etc.) for instance, technical change tends to take the form of the setting up of whole new plants incorporating the latest technology. When workers and all but top managers are introduced to the plant, decisions regarding work organisation may already be largely 'built in' to the plant, and although there may be some choice over exact working practices, that choice may be extremely limited. In these cases it may be most important to concentrate on the *design* of the plant, since it is here where the most important social decisions have been made. In contrast, the automation of batch production is characteristically carried on machine by machine within existing plants, rather than in great leaps and in new locations, and there are thus repeated opportunities for operational managers to choose among alternatives. There is also, of course, the possibility that existing custom and practice will influence the way new equipment is used. Further, batch production tends to be carried on by smaller firms, and the majority of batches are of less than fifty components. Both these points mean automation is more difficult than in other sectors, reinforcing the tendency towards incremental innovation.

Design of Technology

The empirical material gathered in the case studies focuses mainly on the debugging and implementation stage of innovation. However, the vital importance of the design stage must be discussed. Here the recent work by David Noble in America is especially important.[6] Noble traces the design of NC machine tools back to the second world war, and points out that in the initial stages of development there were two types of NC system. One, a 'record-playback' system, involved the machinist making the first of a batch of components in the conventional way, using the machine's manual controls. An electronic control device would record all the movements made by the operator so that the rest of the batch would run automatically. The second type, what is now conventional NC, involves the preparation of a paper tape by programmers by encoding in 'machine-readable' form the instructions for the movements of the machine tool. With this system, at least theoretically, the operator simply has to load and unload the machinery and monitor its movements – the rest is automatic. According to Noble there were no convincing economic advantages in favour of either system over the other. Rather, the second type was developed out of social and political considerations – that is, this system meant that control over the quantity and quality of production could be taken out of the hands of the skilled machinists on the shopfloor, and placed in the hands of programmers. Programmers were assumed to be more management-oriented and thus less problematic to deal with. Any de-skilling effects which NC systems have are thus related less to 'technical necessities' than to an attempt by managers and engineers involved in their design to take control from a problematic workforce.

More recently, with the development of CNC and the proliferation of variations in the detailed design of control systems, adopting firms have more choice over the use to which they put NC.[7] Of particular interest here is some current research being carried out at the Machine Tool Division of the University of Manchester Institute of Science and Technology. Howard Rosenbrock, John Boon and others have begun to examine the possibilities of designing an NC system for operator programming on the shopfloor. The research team includes sociologists as well as engineers, and the strong *moral* component of the work is very encouraging. Already, an NC lathe which is programmed at the machine's own control computer has been successfully demonstrated, and in fact is claimed in many respects to be economically superior to existing alternatives. The intention now is to extend the control system to a whole 'flexible manufacturing system' (FMS), which involves a robot as well as two machine tools. The hope is to allow the development of a 'computer-aided craftsman' rather than reduce the operator to a semi-skilled machine minder – a point we will return to when discussing the fate of traditional craft skills in the final chapter. Most excitingly, at the same time as the more ambitious experiments with FMSs go on, commercial backers are being sought for the prototype lathe in industry, and we must now await the response.

As we shall see, with NC and other applications of electronic controls to batch production processes, adopting firms still have to choose between alternative designs, and even then important decisions have to be made on the organisation of work around the technology. However, for some computer applications relevant to batch engineering, the design of the system allows little flexibility in organisation. Our study of the computerisation of a production control system provides a good example. Here the reallocation of the tasks of the progress clerks from functional area to section area meant that all the skill and knowledge, and the integrity and satisfaction in work that go with it, have been eliminated. Instead of chasing all the parts necessary for the building of a machine or group of machines, the clerk now simply arranges for the work in his section of the machine shop to be allocated in the order dictated by a computer print-out. There can be no doubt that alternative, more interesting and varied, systems could have been 'computerised', and indeed the firm has now tacitly acknowledged this with recent considerations of another system with very different implications. Enid Mumford, among others, has focused on computerised administrative systems, and in particular has looked at the way the values (or 'models of man') employed by computer systems designers can influence the type of work they create for the users of new systems.[8]

In cases such as these, where administrative and control systems are 'computerised', the political mechanisms (and thus the policy implications) are very different. In particular, there is a more direct relationship between the intentions of the designer and the nature of work of the system users – in fact designers often have to work intimately with the adopting firm in order to assess their specific needs. As opposed to most instances of the design of new control devices for batch machinery – where the designer may be more remote both geographically and in time – designers are present and working during 'adoption', and can thus be influenced in important ways directly. It is not surprising then, that Mary Weir has been able to talk about how new computer systems can 'reinforce existing hierarchies' within firms – those in positions of senior power can directly influence designers.[9]

Choice of Technology

The official criteria for choice between alternative machinery on the market were, as we have already pointed out, highly technical. Reference was made in great detail to costs, suitability to production needs, payback periods, productivity gains, and so on. However, it became clear during the studies that choices among alternative options were frequently coloured by considerations of the type of work they implied and, relatedly, the control issues involved.

For instance, in the case of the machine tool manufacturer, production engineers, superintendents and higher managers were divided on whether to move in the direction of operator-programmable CNC machine tools (MDI), or to remain with conventional CNC machine tools. The choice, it was clear, was essentially a *social* one between shopfloor control over production (MDI machine tools) or office control (conventional CNC), and it is worth repeating the quote from the production engineer who summed up the options: 'The firm has to go one of two ways. We can either retain skill on the shopfloor and have manual data input, or transfer skill into here with more tape control machines'. The different positions taken up by the various actors were clearly a reflection both of the politics of the workplace, and of the values of the individuals involved. In particular, there was a division between superintendents and foremen on the shopfloor who were in favour of MDI, and some engineers and top managers who had a strong preference for anything which would take control away from the operators.[10] The superintendents and foremen were certainly motivated by their objective interests in that shopfloor control also meant the retention of managerial control in their hands. However, their stand on the issue was also a reflection of the moral value they placed on craft skills. Being skilled machinists themselves, they identified strongly with the plight of the skilled worker subject to de-skilling technology, and viewed any possibilities for retaining skills with sympathy. Some engineers saw conventional CNC as an opportunity to extend their influence within the firm, but with programming staff attempting to incorporate as much responsibility as possible for pre-production functions into their own domain, the engineers recognised the dangers of programmers attempting to usurp their own traditional roles. Relevant higher managers in the firm, being mostly recent recruits, were still developing their views at the time the research was carried out, and in any case little direction had been offered by previous management teams. The choices to come, however, were clearly going to be influenced strongly by the new top managers, and also by the new American parent company, which was already making its influence felt in other areas. Unfortunately what happens next is unknown, but the important point has been made – that choice of technology is dependent on social values and political interests.

In the plating firm, with the small management team openly adopting a de-skilling strategy, the equipment was chosen with this end unambiguously in mind. In fact, the firm was even able to instruct the machine control system suppliers to *install* the system with this end in mind. The control panels for the plating process were located in a separate room so that only managers could alter them, and thus direct management control over quantity and quality of production could be secured. Thus control was sought through isolation and separation.

These two examples from the machine tool manufacturer and the plating company serve to show how the choice of technology is coloured by politics. Finally, however, we should mention the optical company where the choice of equipment, which tended to be de-skilling in its consequences, appeared not to have an overt social or political dimension. The firm simply acquired 'the latest'. It is difficult to say how much more discretion managers could have exercised in their choices – perhaps they could have persuaded the machine manufacturers to design to alternative specifications. But even assuming that it was very limited, one can still point to the design of the technology (which may be out of the hands of the managers of this firm but is nonetheless subject to change by someone) and to the establishment of a work organisation around the technology (and here managers did impose their values) as junctures at which innovations could be influenced.

Implementation and Debugging

When new electronic control devices are applied to manufacturing processes, important implications for the nature of work tend to be 'built in' to the machinery. As Noble and Rosenbrock point out, social choices have already been made during design. Generally the automated process has been designed *in isolation from* the particular plant adopting the innovation, without reference to that plant's peculiar existing organisational arrangements – the payment system in operation, established working practices, etc. Thus to some extent the technology *will* be external and have 'impacts'. However, there is in most instances still a good deal of 'organisational choice' available, and the impacts depend very much on the use made of the machinery.

The most important point about the implementation and debugging of production technology is that it is at this stage, at least as far as batch production is concerned, where people on the receiving end of technological advance – i.e., workers – can most seriously attempt to impose their own interests.

Working practices in the machine tool manufacturing firm had evolved in favour of the operators over a period of a few years. Here, as we have stated above, there was some dispute as to whether control of production should be in the hands of programmers or operators. There was a 'battle for control' between the interested parties, carried on with each new batch of components. As has been made clear, during the research period the operators were generally winning the battle, being in a position to choose when (and when not) they wished to carry out their own editing, or occasionally even programming. The support of operators by foremen and superintendents meant that programmers would find the appropriation of the editing function extremely difficult unless there was a significant change of policy implemented by higher management – a point recognised by the programmers themselves.

In the plating and rubber moulding firms, by contrast, management expressed a clear preference for using electronic controls in order to shift control of production to the office, where managers (in the case of the plating company) or process control staff (in the case of the rubber moulding company) could predetermine the movements of the machinery. In both cases, however, workers succeeded in imposing their own interests, and the working practices which evolved were not to management's designs. This was mainly because during the implementation of the new processes operators were able to become involved in the establishing of work methods with the new equipment. In the plating company, for instance, during the debugging of the new control systems, it was necessary to make occasional use of a manual override until the computer programmes were perfected. Operators *still* use the manual override, however, in order to control both their own work pace and the quality of finish on goods. Now that 'debugging' is almost complete, these practices have already become to some extent institutionalised, and managers have had to revert to the old styles of supervision in order to maintain management controls and standards.

In the case of the rubber moulding firm, which found similar unwanted working practices becoming institutionalised during debugging, the next set of machinery to be introduced will be 'productionised' (their phrase) away from the shopfloor in a separate development area.[11] Only when machinery is ready for full-scale and uninterrupted production will workers see it. The time-study man can then time the job with work methods *pre-arranged* by development staffs, and the operator will have no say in the establishment of standards. In effect, only management interests will be 'built in' to the work organisation. Thus the new development area represents an attempt by management to incorporate their perceived interests into the technical organisation of the factory at the expense of the workers' interests. Designed on the basis that working practices will now be a matter for management choice only, the new development area, in a very important sense, has its own politics.[12] The evolution of working practices then, provides a direct feedback to design considerations and, of course, to the 'choice of technology' stage, strongly influencing future decisions.

The various stages of innovation described above provide junctures at which people intervene to influence the process of technical change and its effects. In fact they provide opportunities for social policy making, albeit normally unacknowledged, which have profound influences on the nature of work. On the basis of our findings, we will now turn our attention to some of the policy issues which are raised, and how they might better be dealt with in the future.

10 Policy Implications

Despite the current popularity of New Technology Agreements,[1] bargaining over skills and the organisation of work remains at an unofficial, often covert level. There are three main reasons for the informality of negotiations over work organisation. The first and most immediate reason is that skills and job tasks are traditionally not an agenda item in normal collective bargaining.[2] We return to this point in detail later in the chapter. The second reason relates to the more general and obvious point that organisations face a radically new situation with the introduction of microelectronic control devices – the uncertainty which arises cannot be dealt with within existing organisational arrangements or power structures. As Bacharach and Lawler[3] point out, where a situation of uncertainty exists within organisations, informal influence networks are likely to provide the dynamics of change. The formal power given by office only provides resistance. It is only later that influence relationships may 'undergo institutionalisation, acquire legitimacy, and re-emerge as authority relationships'.[4] During the process of change informal politics are at the forefront. The third reason is related to the second. As chapter nine made clear, innovation is shrouded by the ideology of efficiency, and frequent appeal is made to this ideology, especially by managers, in order to preserve or create desired organisational arrangements. The grounds on which choices are *really* made may thus be concealed, and negotiations carried on without ideologies being 'on the table' (acknowledged and considered).

The apparent anarchy of decision-making which all this implies makes it all the more urgent that the real policy issues are faced, and that organisations approach the new technology with a fuller understanding of its implications and possibilities. We will now address ourselves to these policy issues.

Skills and Training

One of the most important aspects of new technology is the fate of skills under its influence. Claims that computerisation de-skills regardless of the social context have been made, and so have claims that the new technology inevitably de-skills so long as the context of its introduction is capitalism (see chapter one). The contribution of the case studies to the skills debate is (i) that technology is not autonomous and therefore *does not* have impacts regardless of the social context, and (ii) that forces of competition do not necessarily impel firms to impose specific skill structures. Rather, it was shown that the technical and social organisation of work – and thus *a range of applied* skills – is a negotiable phenomenon, determined by social and political processes whose outcomes are never certain.

In the case of electronic and computer control of batch production, the major issue is the 'transfer' of skill from work on the machine itself to work with programmes or process controls, and it is frequently commented that conceptual skills come to dominate in place of declining traditional manual skills. The notion that this necessarily entails the de-skilling of the operator, and the creation of a new elite of programmers or process controllers, however, was repeatedly shown in the case studies to be an unfounded assumption. Certainly some firms – especially the plating company and the rubber moulding company – set out with this intention. But even here workers succeeded to some extent in retaining skills on the shopfloor. In the machine tool manufacturer, some operators even went so far as to carry out their own programming, using the tape editing facility, at the machine itself. Management policies and worker responses, therefore, were shown to be centrally important in determining the skill structures of individual firms, and at this 'micro' level general explanations in terms of technology and/or the wider social and economic context were of little value in themselves.

All this is not to undermine the value of analyses which make reference to the rates of diffusion of innovations, general labour market trends, and so on, but it is to question their use in explanations of events within individual firms. In particular, for the purposes of national training programmes, it is difficult to see how aggregate level analyses can be avoided, and certainly they are likely to expose the existence of particular trends – e.g., in skill shortages or gluts – which might not otherwise be identified. But the identification of skills problems and possible training policies for individual firms *must* take into account the political processes involved, and even at a national level a clear understanding of the processes behind the figures is helpful. Indeed, there may be some interaction between national training programmes and job design within individual firms, since management may take skills availability into account when designing their jobs, and workers' existing skills will influence the degree of control they wish to exercise. National training bodies thus need not be merely adaptive, for if workers take to the workplace a set of skills and knowledge about the processes therein, they are more likely to attempt to exercise them. Thus, for instance, in the rubber moulding firm where operators had spent many years as semi-skilled workers with limited responsibility, it was a relatively simple matter for managers to 'buy off' any control which workers exercised on the new machinery. In contrast, operators in the machine manufacturing firm stubbornly refused to give up control of production in the face of pressure from programmers, their defence being based on the tradition of craft skills which they were reluctant to see unused.

Our central concern was with the way skill structures were generated on the shopfloor – i.e., within firms. Here, Enid Mumford, among others, has pointed out that skilled machinists *could* be trained in programming, so that the whole machining process remains in their hands,[5] and the same holds true for the other batch production processes which were the subject of our case studies. Howard Rosenbrock has made a nonsense of the idea that the old and new skills are not compatible, and the possibilities with the new technology are summed up in his image of the 'computer-aided craftsman'.[6] Instead of designing and using new control systems to de-skill workers, they can be designed specifically as 'tools' to aid craftsmen just as computers may be used by doctors to aid their diagnoses. Indeed, we found in our case study firms examples of individual operators in effect training themselves in programming and process control, and the formal recognition and establishment of these working practices would be a simple matter. De-skilling strategies were, however, more dominant than others, and it would take something of a shift in political stance among managers to change this situation.[7] In the meantime, operators will continue to seek to exercise their skills and maintain control, albeit mainly in unorganised and subterranean ways.

Thus, within the broad traditions of the de-skilling, fragmentation and degradation of work, among the details of working practices, we find alternative modes of work – for instance the plating line operator using the manual override, the optical company manager encouraging the rotation of jobs, etc. Occasionally these practices may become institutionalised, developing as viable alternatives and representing a new tradition of skill enhancement – operator programming of machine tools providing perhaps the best example our case studies uncovered. Redirecting technology along more human lines is a matter of nurturing and developing these new traditions, rather than seeing them as a subversive threat and seeking to eliminate them at the next technological opportunity – for example by removing the manual override from the plating line, or using computer-aided design to by-pass machine tool tape editing.

(Research into new technology and skills is now continuing in the University of Aston's Technology Policy Unit in collaboration with the Manpower Services Commission.)

Social Choices for Managers and Engineers

For managers who would wish to continue to de-skill and demean workers, this book is probably of little use. It has little to say to them, and in any case managers and engineers are well practised in justifying political decisions on so-called 'objective' grounds – the book will not help them there. Rather, it is hoped that some managers may better see their own role with the introduction of new technology, and the alternative strategies available to them.

There already exists a good deal of managerial literature on 'job design', 'job enrichment', etc.,[8] and in turn this has been criticised by a host of radicals on the grounds that in practice, redesigning jobs is carried on only to the extent that it is profitable and/or maintains or extends the control of a capitalist class.[9] Thus Tom Lupton and his colleagues, in a review of job design experiments across Europe, could comment that:

> The process of 'humanising the work' has . . . mostly been a means to an end, rather than the end itself. The "end" has variously been a need for production flexibility, to attract labour, to avoid revolutionary protest, or response to trades-union pressure, all with economic survival and/or development in mind.[10]

However, it is surely a one-dimensional view which sees managers at work as solely concerned with profits, just as it is a one-dimensional view which sees workers as solely concerned with payment. The machine tool firm was enlightening on this point – contra profits, different sections of management were shown to hold different values and ideals, which were translated into demands for corresponding forms of work organisation on the shopfloor. Attempts to humanise work, or to maintain or extend skills, may be political in motivation, and managers' political inclinations may be informed from sources other than the abstract interests of capital.

Beryl Tipton summarises the political qualities of job restructuring. They are qualities which business school lecturers might bear in mind:

> Changes in job content, other than of the most trivial kind, require the restructuring of traditional hierarchies of occupational prestige and control. . . . A significant policy to improve the quality of working life even at workplace level is inevitably *a complicated social and political undertaking*: one that could not be accomplished without *a commitment to the value of equality and a greater belief*

that talent is quite widely distributed among the population than is apparent from current practice.[11]

Here we might again emphasise that the 'interests of capital' are not necessarily the determining influence, as Braverman would have it. Certainly all our evidence suggests that most of the important decisions about technology – from its choice to the establishment of detailed working practices – are taken deeply within organisations. Owners may sanction capital investment proposals which come from within organisations, and they may demand that certain levels of profitability are maintained; but this research provided no evidence that de-skilling manpower policies were connected in any immediate sense to these demands. To the contrary, appeals to efficiency, profitability, etc., were shown almost invariably to act primarily as justifications, not determinants. Thus engineers and managers do have the scope to maintain and extend skills, and the indications are that the degree of discretion available is sufficient to allow for considerable variations in the technical and social organisation of work.

However, while we hold out the possibility of a more socialist management with regard to work organisation – and our case studies verify that possibility – we should also emphasise the vital role which trade unions might play. After all, some will still, perhaps justifiably, find it '. . . hard to believe that substantial changes involving the erosion of management's own position, which is implied in this argument, would be initiated by management itself'.[12] We will comment on trade union involvement in the final section of this chapter.

Finally, we might repeat once again that one of the major obstacles which managers – and especially personnel and training managers – must overcome is the 'engineers supply the technology, we deal with the consequences' syndrome. The case studies show how managers *do* mediate in the process of changing technology, both with regard to organisational and technological choices. 'Modernisation' is no excuse for wholehearted de-skilling.

As far as engineers in particular are concerned, there may be no direct, immediate and obvious pressures to design or choose machinery and computer systems in ways which de-skill and make mundane the tasks of those who work with them. Engineers may thus, perhaps innocently, simply not conceive of themselves as advancing political interests on behalf of themselves or the managers of firms taking up the technology. Certainly engineers sometimes *are* highly aware. This was shown to be the case in the machine tool firm, and as outlined in chapter nine, David Noble cites a case where engineers are implicated politically in an immediate sense. More intensive research is needed into machine tool technology and other technologies to see the political processes at work during design.

Where immediate political motivations are *not* uncovered, it is still possible to examine the values or 'models of man' employed by engineers, and here the little research which has been carried out has shown engineers to employ as design criteria a woefully pessimistic view of man.[13] More research is needed – especially into the social *processes* of design – before these findings can be acted upon fully, though the *educational* needs of engineers are strikingly obvious.

Bargaining Issues for Trade Unions?

The most interesting issues brought to light by the case studies – those of skills and control – were never bargained over in the traditional sense. Rather, the tendency was for working practices to become established during the implementation and debugging of the technology, and then to be re-negotiated, on a regular basis, sometimes with each new batch of components to be made. Working arrangements would over a period of time become incorporated into the custom and practice of the factory floor. The assumptions and interests of the various parties to the changes, and their particular positions of power within the organisations, were shown to determine outcomes, but rarely was this process of bargaining and accommodation made explicit. The coordination of workers' strategies for control was particularly weak, and worker initiatives remained largely at a subterranean or individual level. In the case of the machine tool manufacturer, shop stewards had occasionally defended individual operators against the encroachments of programmers, but this was only at the specific request of operators on certain occasions, and the steward organisation had no conscious strategy, let alone official policy, on the issues. Our case studies repeatedly made it clear that the strength of subterranean challenges to management designs should never be underestimated, but nonetheless one might expect trade unions to take a more serious interest.

At the national level, trade unions have recognised the need to form policies to deal with the effects of technological change, and there has recently been a flurry of publications on 'the new technology' calling for trade union involvement through collective bargaining and other means.[14] However, so far, official negotiations involving trade unions have tended to focus on issues of payment, redundancy, safety, and so on, and if unions are to come to terms with the issues of control and skills, a major redirection of trade union concerns will be necessary. Current research by Robin Williams and Russell Moseley of the Technology Policy Unit, University of Aston, is focusing on the trade union response to new technology, and their findings should throw some light on the possibilities for a more direct union involvement.[15] There is of course a great difficulty in diffusing new stances on technology to where it counts – in the stewards' organisations within individual firms. But this is the only place where effective bargaining on the issues can take place. The rapidly rising importance of the shop stewards' movement in recent years[16] should be taken advantage of, and the task now at hand is to secure effective steward involvement.

Over ten years ago Hugh Scanlon summarised the major problems of dealing with technical change:

> So what is involved here? The main and most immediate objective which is the starting point for industrial democracy is to oppose the position where organised labour can only react to management decisions and fight a difficult rearguard action to reduce the magnitude of their impact. It must be recognised that conventional collective bargaining systems are not appropriate for dealing with technological changes, particularly when . . . planning has been reduced from decades to months. It is no longer possible or desirable to wait for the end of a specific contract period to negotiate, when management's decisions are already and quite arbitrarily in the pipeline. These decisions may threaten technological unemployment, obsolescence of skills, disappearance of trades and industries and geographical displacement of the workers themselves. To protect workers adequately, we must be involved with decisions as they occur. We need an anticipatory function at the planning and implementation stages. This is getting to the kernel of our struggle for industrial democracy.[17]

Thus the traditional methods of bargaining are wholly inadequate for technological change. Indeed, in one instance in the case studies where a formal agreement on new technology and working practices was reached by union and management (in the rubber moulding company), it was drawn up *after* the change was implemented, and was concerned solely with matters of pay and effort.[18] The need is for workers' organisations to become involved at the earliest possible stage, and this will involve challenging management's prerogative with regard to decision-making on technology. One instance will suffice: the machinists who currently carry out their own editing of tapes (and occasionally programming) would reinforce their position if unions could persuade management to move in the direction of manual data input machines in favour of conventional, office-programmed machines. By failing to influence these decisions on choice of technology the machinists remain in a precarious position, and a radical change in management's policy on working arrangements could easily mean the transformation of the working practices now established. Unfortunately, shop stewards in the plant simply do not yet see this area of decision-making as their legitimate concern, and indeed only one steward was even fully aware of the difference between MDI and conventional CNC. As is generally the case, the major concern of the union was that any labour displaced by CNC would be reabsorbed elsewhere, and once assurances were gained on this issue, the stewards felt they had had their say. Assuring that labour displacement is minimised is no doubt a vital task for trade unionists. However, as Robert Blauner has pointed out, for the past forty years

> . . . the unions have been mostly concerned with the problem of maintaining the *jobs* of their members, and therefore they have been relatively unconcerned about the *kind of work* their people do. With the realistic fears of unemployment brought about by further technological change, it seems likely that this 'blind spot' in union outlook might continue for another forty years.[19]

Probably the single most useful, and easiest to implement, measure which trade unions could take in order to eliminate their 'blind spot' would be to make frequent use of thorough research into the specific implications of all new technology introduced into plants. Perhaps they could even attempt to justify alternative production machinery in order to influence the direction of change before certain constraints are imposed. This book hopefully points to the areas which such research should seek to illuminate. The stewards' organisation is frequently well established. The problem is one of developing an acute awareness of new technology at the earliest possible stage.

Appendix Research Methods and Methodological Problems

Methods

The primary methods of research were:

(i) Interviews with the various interested parties.

(ii) Observation of working methods and practices; and discussion of these methods on the job with managers and workers.

(iii) Examination of documented information.

(iv) Observation of meetings relevant to the choice of technology and negotiation of change.

There is no clear preference for any of these methods of data acquisition over the others, and the original intention was to use all the methods to the fullest extent. Of course, this was not possible in all cases for various reasons, and whatever sources of information were made available were considered. Occasionally information gained on important points was suspect, but where used the fact is made clear in the presentation of the case studies.

For the most part, once initial access was established (the general problem of access is discussed below), the case studies involved arriving at the firm in order to conduct a pre-arranged interview with a senior manager, and later attempting to persuade the manager to allow interviews to be conducted with other managers and workers within the organisation. In some cases the confidence of one or more managers was gained, and the gathering of information spread from there into the lower echelons of the organisation. *Specific* problems of access to certain sources of information were met as they came along. As in all social research, the data were in some ways incomplete, but in the four detailed case studies it was felt that a reliable and adequate data base was established.[1]

Since the case studies were longitudinal – i.e., they covered events over a period of time rather than presented 'snapshots' of the organisation – revisits were necessary over long periods. Unfortunately, the period of research was generally too short to cover all the various stages of innovations, from design to trial to implementation to debugging and so on, and thus post hoc accounts of events were occasionally relied upon. Similarly, in at least one case (the rubber moulding firm) the research had to end before the 'story' was complete. Without extending a research project over at least several years, little can be done about this problem of time-scale. However, these problems are more than compensated for by the detail which this type of work allows, and besides, the implementation and debugging phases – our major concern – were generally well covered in the research.

Interviews were the major source of data, and occasional discretionary use was made of a tape recorder. Questions to be put to interviewees were generally determined prior to the interview, but interviews were mainly open-ended in an attempt to record the views and perceptions of the respondents. Familiarity with some of the actors involved, especially in the case study of the machine tool manufacturer, meant that eventually conversations came to replace formal 'interviews' with some participants, and the research could almost have been described as 'participant' observation.

Initial interviews with senior managers were used to gain a knowledge of the background of the company – size, product market, management structure, and so on – and also to gain an account of relevant technical changes from their perspective. Interviews and meetings with other relevant actors would then be focused on specific aspects of the innovations as they related to the actors' own perceived interests. In this way the important events within firms came to light, and specific features of innovations could be followed up in detail with the various interested parties.

Observing the working methods used by the various sections of the workforce was often the easiest way of coming to terms with the specific implications of technical change. Most people are in any case starved of opportunities to discuss their work, and a serious listener was in most instances welcomed. Apart from recording details of methods, it was also possible to gain insights into workers' views of technical change, and the specific preferences for working practices which they had.

Documented information was often difficult to acquire, and managers normally wished to vet the information which they were willing to pass on – the excuse almost invariably being that the issues were highly 'sensitive'. The two most valuable types used were (i) formal justifications for expenditure on capital equipment, and (ii) written agreements on manning levels, working practices and payment systems associated with new technology. Use of both these sources of information, however, was problematic, as we will discuss below.

Finally, observing relevant formal meetings was rarely allowed, and provided no important data even though its potential to do so appeared great. Again, we will discuss this shortly.

Methodological Problems

Taking the use of documented information first: formal written justifications for expenditure on capital equipment tended to be highly technical, and gave the impression that choice of technology was of interest only to production engineers. The final decision or recommendation was virtually always in terms of the technology's economic advantages – payback periods, etc. Yet interviews *even with the engineers responsible for writing justifications* almost invariably revealed some social and political dimensions to the decision. The written justification, then, was in part a *scientific gloss* which might crumble when examined at all closely, and its use as empirical evidence of the motivations behind changes, without the support of solid observational and interview material, is likely at the best to be inaccurate, and at the worst misleading. This does not mean that *all* technical decisions *necessarily* incorporate overt social and political elements – but it does mean that the ones which do not are likely to be naive – as managers and engineers are likely to find out later when the social consequences of their decisions are revealed.[2]

Similarly, formal written agreements on aspects of new technology were of little use by themselves. These were in any case rare, and where they did exist they normally concentrated on issues of pay and redundancy. Where working practices *were* specified – for instance in the rubber moulding company – there were normally important divergences from the written agreement. Only by examining the day-to-day interactions of workers and managers could working practices be properly understood. Apart from this necessary incompleteness of formal agreements on working practices, they also fail, of course, to give any indication of either the motives of the various interest groups in attempting to achieve particular forms of work organisation, or the power positions of these groups. Thus in general, most of the qualitative information required was not on record, and where it was it could be used only in the context of more reliable interview and observational evidence.

Observing meetings was rarely allowed by managers, again on the grounds of 'sensitivity', and for the most part second-hand accounts had to suffice. Since most formal worker-management meetings on new technology concentrated, in any case, on pay and redundancy (normally slightly increased pay grades and guarantees of no redundancy) this was no great loss. However, meetings between managers themselves, where issues of supervision and control were discussed, could have proved invaluable sources of data. Occasionally *informal* 'meetings' developed in my presence during the machine tool manufacturer case study – especially between superintendents and foremen – and these, more than any source, clarified for me the various interests and power positions of different groups of managers. But it was not possible to observe the same in the highest reaches of management, where for the most part interviews had to suffice. This was part of the general problem of access to people in positions of authority – what Colin Bell has called the problem of 'studying up'[3] – and represents one of the major limitations of the case study approach. There is no simple answer to this problem, but in retrospect it might be said that I could have displayed more confidence, and certainly the advice to anyone else contemplating intensive methods where senior managers are involved, is to take this problem seriously into account – perhaps enlisting the practical support of more senior academics. In general however access was excellent, and this was due in part to the involvement of two such people during the pilot studies.

Notes and References

Chapter 1

1 A very brief introduction to the meaning and uses of 'microchip technology' can be found in Department of Industry, *Microelectronics: the New Technology* (London: HMSO, 1978). For a more detailed discussion of the development and applications of microelectronics see E. Braun and S. MacDonald, *Revolution in Miniature* (Cambridge: Cambridge University Press, 1978).

2 See E. Braun, *The Dilemma of Automated Production* (Technology Policy Unit, University of Aston, Unpublished paper, 1978).

3 E. Braun, *Technological Change and Unemployment* (Technology Policy Unit, University of Aston, Unpublished paper, 1978).

4 D. Bell, *The Coming of Post-Industrial Society* (New York: Basic Books, 1973).

5 J.I. Gershuny, *After Industrial Society?* (London: Macmillan, 1979).

6 C. Jenkins and B. Sherman, *The Collapse of Work* (London: Eyre Methuen, 1979).

7 A comprehensive discussion of the more general employment issues associated with the new technology is found in R. Rothwell and W. Zegveld, *Technical Change and Employment* (London: Frances Pinter, 1979).

8 R. Blauner, *Alienation and Freedom* (Chicago: University of Chicago Press, 1964).

9 J.R. Bright, *Automation and Management* (Boston: Harvard Business School, 1958).

10 For a summary of the different effects of automation in each of these sectors see J. Child, 'Technical Progress' in B. Barrett et al. (eds.), *Industrial Relations and the Wider Society* (London: Collier Macmillan, 1975), pp.144–162.

11 Science Research Council, Working Party Report, 'NC Machine Tool Systems', in *Colloquium on Robotics*, Paper No.8 (Glasgow, National Engineering Laboratory, 30–31 March 1978).

12 This is no longer simply because microelectronics makes the machines significantly cheaper – most control systems are already only a small part of the total cost of a machine tool – but because they will facilitate the development of more powerful NC systems.

13 The technical problems associated with NC technology are discussed in S.K. Bhattacharyya, *Penetration and Utilisation of NC/CNC Machine Tools* (Science Research Council, Engineering Board, Manufacturing Technology Committee Working Party Report, November 1976). The major *non-technical* reasons for the failure of the UK engineering industry to take up NC on a significant scale are to do with the quality of British management. See N. Swords-Isherwood and P. Senker, 'Automation in the Engineering Industry', *Labour Research*, vol.67, no.11, November 1978, pp.230–231, where a comparison of the attitudes of British and German management and engineers is made. German managers cope better, they suggest, due to their superior organisation, training and education.

14 Traditionally a 16% utilisation rate for machine tools has been considered good and even slight improvements on that figure make good economics. Utilisation rates of around 60% are often claimed for NC systems. See P. Marsh, 'Towards the Unmanned Factory', *New Scientist*, 31 July 1980, pp.373–377. A full discussion of NC costs and the problem of utilisation is found in S.K. Bhattacharyya, *op. cit.* His survey of seventy companies found only 5% of firms 'fully exploiting' NC, and he recommends better organisation of support functions (maintenance, tooling, production control, etc.) in order to improve utilisation.

15 A detailed discussion of the technical advantages of CNC over NC is found in N.C. Ferguson, 'A History of Numerically Controlled Machine Tools', *Chartered Mechanical Engineer*, September 1978, pp.89–92.

16 A technical description of some of the latest CNC systems is found in P. Marsh, 'A Fresh Start for British Machine Tools', *New Scientist*, 26 February 1981, pp.544–546. This article is especially interesting since it comments on the state of British machine tool control system design.

17 A good, if rather over-dramatic, overview of microelectronic applications in batch production can be found in Conference of Socialist Economics, Microelectronics Group, *Capitalist Technology and the Working Class* (London: CSE Books, 1980), chapter 6. Other chapters give outlines of applications in other sectors.

18 Remmerswaal's arguments are summarised by R. Rothwell and W. Zegveld, *op. cit.*

19 This point is made clear by N. Swords-Isherwood and P. Senker (eds.), *Microelectronics in the Engineering Industry, the Need for Skills* (London: Frances Pinter, 1980), chapter 9.

20 The blatantly negative physical and social consequences of shiftwork for many people are well documented. See for instance I.I. Wedderburn, *Are Shiftworkers Supermen?* (Paper given at the Annual Meeting of the British

Association for the Advancement of Science, 3–7 September 1979).

21 E. Christensen, *Automation and the Workers* (London, Labour Research Publications, 1968), part 1.

22 N. Swords-Isherwood and P. Senker (1978 and 1980), *op. cit.*

23 The innovation theorists discussed in this section were identified as a 'school of thought' by my colleague Harry Scarbrough. Classic texts from this school include E. Mansfield, *The Economics of Technological Change* (New York: Norton, 1968), N. Rosenberg (ed.), *The Economics of Technological Change* (Harmondsworth: Penguin, 1971); and K. Norris and J. Vaisey, *The Economics of Research and Technology* (London: Allen and Unwin, 1973).

24 E. Mansfield, *op. cit.*, p.99.

25 See for instance C. Freeman, *The Economics of Industrial Innovation* (Harmondsworth: Penguin, 1974), pp.161–197, and, Cabinet Office, Advisory Council for Applied Research and Development (ACARD), *Industrial Innovation* (London: HMSO, 1978). It should be emphasised here that scientific and technical endeavour is generally assumed to be neutral. Research *priorities* may be affected by institutional interests, and the *order* in which advances occur. But the quality of output is held to be independent of any political interests.

26 For example see L. Nabseth and G.F. Ray, *The Diffusion of New Industrial Processes* (Cambridge: Cambridge University Press, 1974).

27 See E. Mansfield, *op. cit.*, chapter 5.

28 A. Touraine, *Workers' Attitudes to Technical Change* (Paris: OECD, 1965).

29 OECD International Seminars 1966/5, *Adjustment of Workers to Technical Change at Plant Level* (Paris: OECD, 1967). See especially pp.23–40 and pp.95–111.

30 See for instance, R.M. Bell, *Changing Technology and Manpower Requirements in the Engineering Industry* (Sussex: Sussex University Press, 1972).

31 Emma Bird, *Information Technology in the Office: the Impact on Women's Jobs* (Manchester: Equal Opportunities Commission, September 1980).

32 For a summary of this 'technological implications' literature see M. Rose, *Industrial Behaviour, Theoretical Developments Since Taylor* (Harmondsworth: Penguin, 1978), pp.173–233; and D. Silverman, *The Theory of Organisations* (London: Heinemann, 1970), pp.100–109. For my own comments on this work see B. Wilkinson, *Technical Change and Work Organisation* (University of Aston, PhD thesis, 1981), chapter 1.

33 Of course, the various authors within the innovation school are restricted by this limitation to greater or lesser degrees, and a thorough analysis would show their various positions. A recent work which does manage to introduce a good deal of social and political context to 'innovations' is G. Rosegger, *The Economics of Production and Innovation* (Oxford: Pergamon Press, 1980).

34 P.A. Baran and P.M. Sweezy, *Monopoly Capital* (Harmondsworth: Penguin, 1968).

35 H. Braverman, *Labour and Monopoly Capital, the Degradation of Work in the Twentieth Century* (New York: Monthly Review Press, 1974), pp.57–8.

36 *Ibid.*, p.171.

37 Braverman's discussion of machine tools is found in *ibid.*, pp.195–203.

38 *Ibid.*, p.202.

39 See H. Shaiken, 'Numerical Control of Work: Workers and Automation in the Computer Age', *Radical America*, vol.13, no.6, November–December 1979.

40 See. M.J.E. Cooley, 'Taylor in the Office' in R.N. Ottoway (ed.), *Humanising the Workplace* (London: Croom Helm, 1977), pp.65–77. Also see his 'Contradictions of Science and Technology in the Production Process' in H. Rose and S. Rose (eds.), *The Political Economy of Science* (London: Macmillan, 1976), pp.72–95.

41 See Conference of Socialist Economics, Microelectronics Group, *op. cit.*

42 S. Marglin, 'The Origins and Functions of Hierarchy in Capitalist Production' in T. Nichols (ed.), *Capital and Labour, Studies in the Capitalist Labour Process* (London: Fontana, 1980), pp.237–254.

43 The term 'frontier of control' comes from Carter L. Goodrich's *The Frontier of Control* (London: Pluto Press, 1975), which was first published more than fifty years ago.

44 For these and other examples see A. Elger, 'Valorisation and Deskilling, a Critique of Braverman', *Capital and Class*, vol.7, Spring 1979. For a recent Marxist discussion which, as the title of the book implies, recognises the active presence of the working class in a lengthy analysis of the labour process, see R.C. Edwards, *Contested Terrain, the Transformation of the Workplace in the Twentieth Century* (London, Heinemann, 1979).

45 A. Elger, *op. cit.* Also see R. Coombs, 'Labour and Monopoly Capital', *New Left Review*, no.107, 1978, pp.79–96. A recent empirically-based discussion of NC applications by Bryn Jones shows clearly that the deskilling strategy is not universal, and that divisions of labour around the new technology depend upon firms' product markets, pre-existing structures of management control, and upon the traditions, strengths and strategies of the trade unions concerned. See Bryn Jones, 'Destruction or Redistribution of Engineering Skills? The Case of Numerical Control' in S. Wood (ed.), *The Degradation of Work: Skill, Deskilling and the Braverman Debate* (London: Hutchinson, 1982).

46 Thus Palmer has commented: 'Braverman is limited in his understanding of the extent to which working class opposition "defeated" Taylorism and pushed capital to employ more subtle means of control in its quest for authority': quoted from B. Palmer, 'Class, Conception and Conflict: the Thrust for Efficiency, Managerial Views of Labour, and the Working Class Rebellion, 1903–1922', *Review of Radical Political Economy*, vol.7, no.2, 1975, p.7.

47 See for instance A.L. Friedman, *Industry and Labour, Class Struggle at*

Work and Monopoly Capitalism (London, Macmillan, 1977), where management strategies are held to vary between a 'direct control' and a 'responsible autonomy' form.

Chapter 2

1 For an exposition of the various sociological approaches to organisations see G. Burrell and G. Morgan, *Sociological Paradigms and Organisational Analysis* (London: Heinemann, 1979).
2 See for example G.K. Ingham, *Size of Industrial Organisation and Worker Behaviour* (Cambridge: Cambridge University Press, 1970).
3 A. Elger, 'Industrial Organisations: a Processual Perspective' in J.B. McKinlay, *Processing People: Cases in Organisational Behaviour* (London, Holt Rinehart and Winston, 1975), p.94.
4 *Ibid.*, p.96.
5 John Child, 'Organisation Structure, Environment and Performance, the Role of Strategic Choice', *Sociology*, vol.6, no.1, 1972, pp.1–22.
6 P. Senker et al, *Technological Change, Structural Change and Manpower in the UK Toolmaking Industry* (Watford, Engineering Industry Training Board, 1976), p.51.
7 For the most recent contribution see N. Swords-Isherwood and P. Senker (eds), *Microelectronics and the Engineering Industry, the Need for Skills* (London: Frances Pinter, 1980), chapter 9.
8 N. Swords-Isherwood and P. Senker, 'Automation in the Engineering Industry', *Labour Research*, vol.67, no.11, November 1978, p.231.
9 Jeffrey Pfeffer, *Organisational Design* (Illinois, US: AHM Publishing, 1978).
10 *Ibid.*, pp.109–10.
11 See for instance D. Bloor, *Knowledge and Social Imagery* (London, Routledge and Kegan Paul, 1976).
12 Seymour Melman, 'Alternative Criteria for the Design of Means of Production', *Theory and Society*, vol.10, no.3, May 1981, p.335.
13 Langdon Winner, 'Do Artefacts Have Politics?' *Daedalus*, Winter 1980, pp.121–136.
14 David Noble, 'Social Choice in Machine Design: the Case of Automatically Controlled Machine Tools' in A. Zimbalist (ed.), *Case Studies in the Labour Process* (New York: Monthly Review Press, 1979), pp.18–50.
15 E. Braun, R. Moseley and B. Wilkinson, 'Manufacturing Innovation in the West Midlands Materials Forming Industry', *Omega*, vol.9, no.6, 1981, pp.563–570.
16 Simply passing through this area is an experience highly recommended: the train from Birmingham New Street to Wolverhampton is the most comfortable means, but some of the very best views of the industrial landscape can be gained by travelling upstairs on a double decker bus from Birmingham bus station to the terminus at Dudley.

17 A detailed description of the region's industry is found in P.A. Wood, *Industrial Britain, the West Midlands* (Newton Abbott: David and Charles, 1976). For a recent discussion of the region's economic ills see P.A. Wintour, 'The Creation of an Industrial Desert', *New Statesman*, 29 August 1980, pp.7–9.

18 Strictly speaking, the spectacle manufacturing firm was engaged in *unit* production. However, unit and small batch production can for our purposes be categorised together.

Chapter 3

1 A broad discussion of NC machining technology was presented in chapter one.

2 In fact it is now possible to discern what may be a trend towards operator-programmable CNC machines. Incorporating a microprocessor in the machine's own control cabinet, they are programmable at the machine itself, during the production of the first of a batch. This type of system, it seems, is often particularly attractive to the smaller engineering concern because it eliminates the need for expensive back-up facilities – especially a separate programming department. One such machine was used by the machine tool manufacturer, which is discussed in more depth in chapter seven.

3 This fourth case is the subject of our major case study in chapter seven.

Chapter 4

1 Out of the original twenty seven case studies, this was one of only two cases of electronic controls being introduced in the absence of new machinery. Normally the machine manufacturer (the supplier) would do the adding-on. As we shall see, the management were able to take political advantage of this fact.

2 Within the plant there is 'men's work' and 'women's work'. Only men do the actual plating, while the women do the 'jigging and unjigging' – attaching components to be plated to jigs with wires, so that they are ready for the plating processes, and later detaching them. This work is far more monotonous than working on the lines.

3 If there are faults in the finished work – e.g., if the plate is uneven, or if the finish is dull, rectification can be difficult and costly. Occasionally whole batches of components are scrapped because their recovery would cost more than they are worth. This is especially the case with low-precision castings and pressings.

4 This problem has now been rectified simply by welding larger handles to the jigs and barrels so that the carriages can hardly miss them.

5 This is a problem, of course, only from the viewpoint of the assumptions displayed by management – i.e., that workers 'cannot be trusted' and are 'unreliable', etc.

6 If management's ideas and actions have not yet appeared contradictory (and they probably have) they certainly do now. Indeed, before the move the general manager talked about the need to 'attract a better class of labourer' at the same time as the need to 'de-skill the operators'.

Chapter 5

1 'Surfacing' refers to the making of lenses on machines which grind 'blank' lenses to the shape and size prescribed by the optician. Including the supervisor and an apprentice, there are seven surfacers.
2 The actual programming for this job is highly complex, and the firm has to use a highly qualified consultant, who works in conjunction with the production manager.
3 Glazing refers to the cutting of lenses to shape, then 'ramming' then into spectacle frames. About twenty two workers are employed in glazing. There are a mixture of men and women, whereas in surfacing, all are men.
4 This is not a criticism in any sense. In fact many of the 'innovators' in other firms shared the same enthusiasm for technology and machinery in themselves – i.e., independently of economic considerations.
5 This is not of course a new finding. There is a whole body of literature which concerns itself with job rotation, job enlargement and job enrichment. For my own comments on this work see chapter two of my PhD thesis, *Technical Change and Work Organisation* (University of Aston, 1981).

Chapter 6

1 Or, more accurately, capacity is slightly higher. Recently the firm has had to impose short-time working due to falling markets.
2 To a large extent through automation, three hundred workers – by way of natural wastage and some redundancy – have been displaced between 1974 and 1980. Important though this point is, the details are beyond the scope of this study.
3 Some works give the impression that there are separate components to 'work organisation' which can be manipulated independently. This is far from empirical reality.
4 'Productionisation' refers to the process of final development and adjustment of machinery to meet the firm's peculiar needs, and to the problem of establishing the new process within the organisation. The term is not invented. It was used liberally by production management and supervision in this case study firm.
5 In this firm, unlike the previous two case studies, more overt and indeed more formal bargaining took place. This finally resulted in a written agreement on the introduction of new technology. One of the main reasons for this more formal approach was no doubt simply the greater size of the firm, but equally, one suspects, it was related to the way the new tech-

nology impinged on the payment system – one of the union's few legitimate concerns.

6 It was claimed to be difficult to convince the men that the new processes were far more 'delicate', and mistakes far more costly. Bad habits on the old presses could be tolerated, but with the new ones 'the whole process has to be just right'.

7 Adjustment of this control is occasionally necessary to prevent blistering or splitting of the rubber components.

Chapter 7

1 It should be emphasised that the latest round of redundancies do not represent a sudden downturn in the fortunes of the company. In fact the company took advantage of the current government's scheme of subsidising short-time working. With the subsidy running out, lay-offs are inevitable. They are the result of a downturn in the market six to twelve months ago.

2 Being 'skilled' is recognised by the company both in terms of status and pay differentials, and as such can hardly be expected to be attributed to, or sought by, individuals or interest groups solely on the grounds of the nature and complexity of their work. Indeed, within this plant at least, 'skilled' has two meanings. Sometimes it refers to the abilities, experience, etc., of the worker, and sometimes simply to an individual's pay grade. The implications for anyone attempting to measure 'skill structures' are obvious.

3 For a wider discussion of the implications of computer-controlled machine tools see chapter one. For the purposes of this chapter we assume a basic knowledge of the nature of CNC.

4 To clarify matters, by 'senior managers' we mean the company's directors plus the personnel manager, and by 'middle managers' we mean all other managers above the level of foreman, including superintendents. Superintendents did in fact play a critical role in the firm, which made a nonsense of their relatively low official status and, as they pointed out to me, their salaries.

5 It is tempting to criticise the short-sightedness of union policy on this count, for if they allow real skills to be de-graded, their bargaining position can only suffer, putting the formal recognition of skills in jeopardy in the long term.

6 Of these nine machinists, several are not *formally* qualified. As with many other of the more experienced workers in the plant, this is mainly because the early part of their working lives were around the time of the second world war, when the luxury of formal training recognised by certificates was rare.

7 The office referred to recently became 'Manufacturing Facilities' (an Americanism) and houses production engineers and industrial engineers,

as well as programmers and planners. I was offered a desk there, and found the place a most useful base for examining CNC and shop scheduling – many of the most important actors being located there.

8 In the context of the recent redundancies due to the recession these assurances now seem rather trivial. However, if and when sales do pick up, the firm will no doubt invest in more computer-controlled equipment rather than labour, and thus in the long run the labour-saving effects of the new technology will be realised.

9 Often, when the batch is complete, the operator will make a tape recording of the programme to be stored in the office for future use.

10 Shaiken cites a case where operators would demand they carry on their own editing because they could produce more, and thus increase their bonus pay. See Harley Shaiken, *Computer Technology and the Relations of Power in the Workplace* (Berlin: International Institute for Comparative Social Research, 1980), p.24.

11 Here I must express my thanks to Professor Howard Rosenbrock and John Boon for explaining their work during a visit to Manchester.

12 At the same time as using the machinist's skills, it is claimed that the system is an improvement on conventional CNC in terms of flexibility, efficiency and utilisation – the points on which MDI is normally criticised. See J. Boon et al., *The Development of Operator Programmable NC Lathes* (University of Manchester Institute of Science and Technology, Unpublished paper, 1981).

13 There must of course be some 'market pull'. Here we cannot attempt a full explanation as to exactly how this might work. However, we should emphasise that adopting firms' choices and demands must be important, and it is worth bearing in mind that machine manufacturers often produce to specification.

14 They have, on the other hand, been directly involved in changes in production control, and we will see exactly how in the next chapter.

Chapter 8

1 Progress clerks even have to commence work at 8 a.m. with the rest of the shopfloor, unlike other office workers who start at nine.

2 The schedulers were kind enough to allow me to actually follow them around the machine shop and the offices as they went about their work, thus allowing the build-up of a detailed picture of the nature of their jobs.

3 Given all this, it may appear ironic that the schedulers are using their changing jobs as a justification for upgrading to skilled status. (Previously the AUEW and management had agreed that progress clerks would remain 'semi-skilled' until their jobs changed, and this is the first opportunity of re-grading they have had since then.) The schedulers, however, cannot even persuade the stewards' committee to represent this claim (the stewards' committee wishes to maintain existing differentials) meaning they

have virtually no bargaining power. The schedulers are a little bitter, describing the stewards as 'doing the management's job for them'.

4 Most employees in the firm – from shopfloor operators to foremen to middle management – look back on the old piecework days with some nostalgia, claiming that overall effort was far higher and remuneration much fairer.

5 One wonders whether there will be any real role left for the ratefixers to play.

6 This simple informal banking system was an 'open secret' within the firm – most people knew what was going on, but no one talked about it. One can imagine the confusion I personally suffered until finding out what was happening. This took several months, and even then the detailed workings of the kitty system remained unclear. In particular, the calculations which allowed the stewards to know when the ceiling was reached probably needed the collaboration of others – either ratefixers or production control staff, but I can only guess the mechanisms at work.

7 My own guess, which cannot be proved in any sense, is that if the blue inspection tickets were to be used, then other information which would normally go into the central computer – i.e. information on the variance codes and times – would be omitted. Since the US parent company are to use, and possibly are using, this other information, it would be plain and obvious to them that the white work tickets were being abused in some way – either by not being completed properly, or by not being used as the information input at all. The control of bonus pay by the workers would thus be exposed to the US parents, and this would mean embarrassment for the UK management.

Chapter 9

1 Interestingly, Blackler and Brown have made similar comments on attempts to improve the quality of working life through job redesign schemes. The lack of adequate data, and the existence of other factors which provide competing explanations for changes in labour turnover, productivity, etc. (e.g., the 'Hawthorne effect'), means that the measurement of the social and economic effectiveness of job design schemes is highly problematic. See F.H.M. Blackler and C.A. Brown, *Job Design and Management Control: Studies in British Leyland and Volvo* (Farnborough: Saxon House, 1978), pp.61–63.

2 In several of the case study firms, some workers and lower managers questioned the value of automation of certain processes, and in many instances it would be difficult to prove them wrong on economic grounds. Occasionally managers and engineers would implicitly recognise this by allowing workers to use manual overrides (e.g. in the plating company, and in the machine tool manufacturer). In other words they acknowledged that

conventional methods, at least with regard to certain batches of product, were more appropriate.

3 Here workers did not have to *actively* resist shiftwork. Management simply assumed that in the current context of redundancies and short-time working the introduction of shiftwork for certain machines would be, at the very least, resented by workers.

4 Nonetheless, the ability of workers, even when unorganised, to generate opposing arguments has been demonstrated, and there is no reason why these initiatives could not be extended and formalised by workers' organisations. It is also possible that workers' organisations could attempt to expose the underlying issues involved in technical change, thus bringing the real political aspects of change to the bargaining table. We will return later to these possibilities.

5 As chapter one pointed out, much of the literature on innovation, in using arguments about the need to remain competitive by adopting the most efficient techniques of production, is equally guilty of creating a false picture of consensus. In this sense it can serve as a management ideology or tool.

6 David F. Noble, 'Social Choice in Machine Design: the Case of Automatically Controlled Machine Tools' in A. Zimbalist (ed.), *Case Studies in the Labour Process* (New York: Monthly Review Press, 1979), pp.18–50.

7 For a brief outline of some of the alternative computer control systems for NC now available see P. Marsh, 'A Fresh Start for British Machine Tools', *New Scientist*, 26 February 1981, pp.544–546. The fact that new control systems which do allow for operator programming are now being designed is a point which makes Noble's work appear a little out of date, and research into the social and political dimensions of current design activities is needed. Indeed, one could make a good case for a major research project to examine the whole political history of the design and development of machine tools.

8 See Enid Mumford, 'Human Values and the Introduction of Technical Change' in J. Moneta (ed.), *Information Technology* (Oxford: North Holland, 1978), pp.239–244.

9 See Mary Weir, 'Are Computer Systems and Humanised Work Compatible?' in R.N. Ottaway (ed.), *Humanising the Workplace* (London: Croom Helm, 1977), pp.44–64.

10 Interestingly, the personnel manager (an increasingly influential figure among the top managers) was perhaps the strongest exponent of deskilling, commenting that his job would be easier if he could get the local butcher's boy or a bus driver to operate the machines with very little training, and during one interview with himself and the manufacturing director he questioned both of us on how it might be possible to use the latest equipment to achieve this.

11 It should be pointed out that only in this case was the desire of operators to

have some control over their own working methods connected in any direct sense to *monetary* advantages, and even here one might question whether the amounts of money at stake could *alone* justify the seriousness of the disputes which arose. An exploration of the reasons for such apparently unnecessary 'games' is found in M. Burawoy, *Manufacturing Consent: Changes in the Labour Process Under Monopoly Capitalism* (Chicago: University of Chicago Press, 1979).

12 In both this case and the case of the layout of equipment in the plating company, we can see unambiguously how designs are politically informed, and how political implications are now built into the hardware. Changing the social relations within these factories would involve changing once again the layout of the factory itself. Other examples of political qualities being incorporated into 'artefacts', and a general discussion of this phenomenon, can be found in Langdon Winner, 'Do Artefacts Have Politics?', *Daedalus*, Winter, 1980, pp.121–136.

Chapter 10

1 For a summary of the nature and scope of New Technology Agreements see R. Williams and R. Moseley, *The Trade Union Response to Information Technology*, Paper given to the EEC 'FAST' Conference on The Information Society, Dublin, 18–20 November 1981.

2 This is not the case in Scandinavia, where work organisation is increasingly a subject for discussion in formal worker–management committees. See Josep Bolweg, *Job Design and Industrial Democracy* (Netherlands: Martinus Nijhoff, 1976). However the second two reasons do apply.

3 S.B. Bacharach and E.J. Lawler, *Power and Politics in Organisation* (London: Jossey Bass, 1981).

4 *Ibid.*, p.42.

5 Enid Mumford, 'The Design of Work, New Approaches and New Needs' in J.E. Rijnsdorp (ed.), *Case Studies in Automation Related to the Humanisation of Work* (Oxford: Pergamon Press, 1979), pp.9–17.

6 See for instance H.H. Rosenbrock, *Automation and Society*, Paper given at the workshop on 'Feedback and Synthesis of Linear and Non-linear Systems', Bielefeld/Rome, 22 June to 3 July 1981.

7 That de-skilling strategies reflect political and value positions was most clearly demonstrated in the case of the machine tool manufacturer, where lower managers sided with operator-initiatives to maintain their control and skills in opposition to programmers and more senior managers.

8 For those unfamiliar with this literature a good summary can be found in M. Rose, *Industrial Behaviour: Theoretical Developments Since Taylor* (Harmondsworth: Penguin, 1978).

9 See for instance M. Bosquet, 'The Prison Factory', *New Left Review*, no.73, May–June 1972, pp.23–34.

10 T. Lupton, I. Tanner and T. Schnelle, 'Manufacturing System Design in

Europe' in G.L. Cooper and E. Mumford (eds.), *The Quality of Working Life in Western Europe* (London: Associated Business Press, 1979), p.53.

11 Beryl Tipton, 'The Quality of Training and the Design of Work', *Industrial Relations Journal*, vol.13, no.1, 1982, p.36. My emphasis.

12 *Ibid.*, p.36.

13 See B. Hedberg and E. Mumford, 'The Design of Computer Systems: Man's Vision of Man as an Integrated Part of the System Design Process' in E. Mumford and H. Sackman (eds.), *Human Choice and Computers* (Oxford: North Holland, 1975), pp.31–60.

14 See for instance AUEW (TASS), *Computer Technology and Employment* (Manchester: National Computing Centre Publications, 1979). A review of these publications, and of the official stances of the major trade unions, is found in K. Robins and F. Webster, 'New Technology: a Survey of Trade Union Response in Britain', *Industrial Relations Journal*, vol.13, no.1, 1982, pp.7–26.

15 This research has already thrown up an analysis of the role of New Technology Agreements in negotiations on technology, and a discussion of their limitations can be found in R. Williams and R. Moseley, *op. cit.*

16 A recent report on the shop stewards' movement shows that since the late 1960's both the number of shop stewards and their recognition has risen dramatically. See W. Brown (ed.), *The Changing Contours of British Industrial Relations* (London: Basil Blackwell, 1981).

17 Quoted D. Hull, *The Shop Steward's Guide to Work Organisation* (Nottingham: Spokesman, 1978), p.21.

18 In this instance the agreement represented the 'buying off' of the average earnings which operators had enjoyed during the debugging and implementation of the new technology. The instance was a reflection of the general problem of the channelling of issues into monetary considerations.

19 R. Blauner, *Alienation and Freedom* (Chicago: University of Chicago Press, 1964), p.185–6. Blauner's emphasis.

Appendix

1 A few firms which began as hopeful possibilities for case studies were, after one or two visits, 'closed-off' before further research could be conducted. Fortunately, alternative options were always available throughout this research period, and thus no serious problem was posed.

2 This was the case in the optical company and the rubber moulding company. In both cases managers failed to properly recognise the possible social consequences of new technology until implemented.

3 C. Bell, 'Studying the Locally Powerful, Personal Reflections on a Research Career' in C. Bell and S. Encel (eds.), *Inside the Whale, Ten Personal Accounts of Social Research* (Oxford: Pergamon Press, 1978), pp.14–40.

Index